AUG 2012

DESIGNING ONLINE LEARNING

DESIGNING ONLINE LEARNING

A Primer for Librarians

Sue Alman, Christinger Tomer, and
Margaret L. Lincoln, Editors

 LIBRARIES UNLIMITED

AN IMPRINT OF ABC-CLIO, LLC
Santa Barbara, California • Denver, Colorado • Oxford, England

Library of Congress Cataloging-in-Publication Data

Designing online learning : a primer for librarians / Sue Alman, Christinger Tomer, and Margaret L. Lincoln, editors.
   pages cm
Includes bibliographical references and index.
   ISBN 978–1–59884–637–9 (pbk.) — ISBN 978–1–59884–638–6 (ebook) (print) 1. Web-based instruc-tion—Design. 2. Web-based instruction—Evaluation. 3. Educational technology. 4. Information literacy—Web-based instruction. 5. Electronic information resource literacy—Web-based instruction. 6. Library education—Web-based instruction. 7. Libraries and distance education. 8. School librarian participation in curriculum planning. 9. Academic libraries—Relations with faculty and curriculum. I. Alman, Susan Webreck. II. Tomer, Christinger. III. Lincoln, Margaret L.
LB1044.87.D48   2012
371.33—dc23   2012017614

ISBN: 978–1–59884–637–9
EISBN: 978–1–59884–638–6

16 15 14 13 12   1 2 3 4 5

This book is also available on the World Wide Web as an eBook.
Visit www.abc-clio.com for details.

Libraries Unlimited
An Imprint of ABC-CLIO, LLC

ABC-CLIO, LLC
130 Cremona Drive, P.O. Box 1911
Santa Barbara, California 93116-1911

This book is printed on acid-free paper ∞

Manufactured in the United States of America

To our families for their support and tolerance of our online schedules.

The Tomer Family: Julie, Cait, Will, and Nora
The Alman Family: RJ, Jennie, Chris, and Hoover
The Lincoln Family: Gary, Ben, Ruth, Geoff, Angela, and Arianna

Contents

Preface

My 10 years or so in online education have been an adventure, and one in which I have probably learned more—and more about myself—than ever before. There are more than a few reasons for this, but as I look back I think the main reason is that in the days when I first entered the domain of online education, it was new and largely uncharted territory, and it quickly became clear that many of the old habits and tricks of teaching that had worked in the traditional classroom wouldn't work. Invention was the order of the day, and I was at a point in my life and career where the need to invent, however feeble my inventions proved to be, made the prospect of online education all the more attractive.

What I didn't fully understand when we began planning an online program at the University of Pittsburgh's School of Information Sciences in 2000 was that online education was about further empowering students (by giving them a new array of choices about how, when, and where to learn). Nor did I fully understand that online education was, among other things, a real and constructive threat to an educational order that was characterized by old hierarchies, smug complacency, and more than a little intellectual stagnation. The realization that online education was something genuinely new and important came slowly—I am, in general, discouragingly slow on the uptake—but I know that it began—the realization, that is—in the summer of 2001. When our program's first cohort of students came to campus for a few days about midway through their first term, it became clear that they had formed strong personal bonds in a matter of eight weeks, working separately and together in an online learning environment (supplemented by the use of various personal technologies, most notably cell phones). It also became clear that there were dimensions to this process that didn't occur in face-to-face classrooms and that could not be duplicated in traditional education settings. More than 10 years on, I am not appreciably better at articulating what I saw and felt when those students came together for the first time, save to say that it convinced me that online education represented an opportunity to break out of old, tired molds and get about the challenging business of rethinking how best to educate people.

Finally, I have learned that, even in the midst of an overbearing educational bureaucracy, one person can make a real difference in the life of a program, and that compassion, decency, and a genuine commitment to the best interests of students can transcend limits of all sorts and overcome almost any problem.

Nothing in the chapters that follow will tell you that, in the midst of all the technologies and learning theories and discussion boards, what matters most is that programs be led by teachers like my colleague, Sue Alman.

—Christinger Tomer

ಬಿಂಬಿ

Through my involvement in online education for the past 11 years, I have discovered one truth that is unfailing for anyone, instructor or teacher, who is also a parent. The minute that you sit down at the computer, one or more of your children will always want you to do something for them! I firmly believe that there is a magnetic attraction between a parent and a child (no matter the age!) that increases when the parent is seated in front of the computer screen.

When I first became involved in online education, the technology included a rudimentary learning management system that worked well enough while I was on campus. In those days, though, most of us had one computer at home with a dial-up connection. The problem of child-interruptus was compounded by the fact that someone else in the family always needed to use the computer or make a call on the landline, or that the connection was so slow that you could walk 20 miles and the file still hadn't loaded.

Since those days, we have progressed to at least one laptop connected to a wireless network for each person in the family, and there is an abundance of other communication devices lying about. Yet all of these "tools" still don't alleviate the interruptions to assist someone with something or "loan" the laptop for "just a minute because mine is in the next room!" I just want you to know that you can be an effective online educator in spite of these obstacles.

About 15 years ago, many prospective adult students told us they wanted to earn the MLIS degree from the University of Pittsburgh but that they were unable to move to Pittsburgh because of work or family obligations. By the year 2000, the technology had finally advanced to a point that we could make plans to develop a fully asynchronous MLIS program at the University of Pittsburgh. Mary Kay Biagini, Christinger Tomer, and I—three kindred spirits—set out into the frontier of online teaching and learning as the student "pioneer cohort" came into existence.

At that time, there were no instruction manuals and precious few experts who could guide us in this process. Undaunted by the task before us, we traveled to the Asynchronous Learning Network conference held at the University of Maryland in College Park to see if we could learn how to develop a fully online program. Our lives changed forever through a serendipitous meeting with Dr. Gene Rubin, chair of the master's in distance education at the University of Maryland University College.

Gene became our mentor and guided us through the conceptual development of our online program. Through his expert guidance, conditions set by the University of Pittsburgh's administration, and our self-taught lessons, we developed, marketed, and launched the program in a six-month period. The online course content was developed at a just-in-time pace, since the instructors and students were treading new paths together.

Throughout the past 11 years, Christinger Tomer's technological expertise has enabled us to try new applications. The courses have transformed, now incorporating not just online asynchronous discussions but a range of multimedia and social media interactions between instructors and students. Chris patiently worked with the instructors and students, who consistently had technology-induced breakdowns! I recommend that you find a collaborator such as Christinger Tomer—it will enrich the experience for yourself and the students.

We want you to know of our struggles and ultimate success, as you may be faced with implementing online learning modules or courses for your user groups. This collection of essays and resources represents the type of information that would have been helpful to us as we began our venture into online education. We have asked people who helped us along the way or who have considerable expertise in their areas to write about best practices in:

- Designing course materials
- Providing faculty resources and instruction
- Becoming familiar with the technology options that are now available
- Assessing the results of those learning online
- Developing information literacy modules for academic settings
- Creating online learning in the K–12 environment

It is our desire to help others who are novices to online learning or who need to update their skills in this rapidly changing environment. While the prospect of becoming involved in online learning can be uncomfortable, we have found it the most rewarding experience of our professional careers, and our teaching philosophy and techniques have changed radically and for the better.

—Sue Alman

಄಄

My involvement in online education came about quite recently in my 39-year career as a school librarian. Upon receiving my AMLS from the University of Michigan's School of Library Science in 1973, I took a position with the Lakeview Public Schools in Battle Creek, Michigan. Though I entered the profession years before the advent of the microcomputer, keeping abreast of technological developments was always important to me. I regularly attended professional development workshops and gained Educational Technology Certification from Michigan State University. In 2004, an opportunity allowed me to update my skills as a library professional while transitioning to the online world. I received a full fellowship to pursue a distance-independent interdisciplinary Ph.D. in information science from the University of North Texas (UNT).

The UNT program aimed to create a diverse cohort of 10 doctoral students, easing monetary, cultural, and geographic roadblocks. Cohort members (selected from among practicing school and public librarians) would eventually fill the ranks of a professoriate needed to train capable, thoughtful, and caring 21st-century librarians. This model for a doctoral program went beyond the traditional brick-and-mortar setting by fostering a blended learning environment of distance education and on-site interaction.

Over a two-year period, cohort members traveled to Denton, Texas, to begin coursework during weekend institutes and then returned home to continue with follow-up assignments and participation in an online content management system. Strong and lasting bonds among cohort members and faculty were established face-to-face and on-line. Together we discovered that with web technology and an abundance of vast educational resources, learning could take place 24/7. The workload was intense, and cohort members faced the further challenge of holding down full-time job responsibilities while enrolled in the program. Yet the first cohort was a success, and a second cohort was similarly funded and formed in 2005.

At an age when many colleagues are thinking of retirement, I proudly earned my degree and was motivated to seek additional ways to be involved online learning initiatives. I taught online for the School of Library and Information Science at San José State University and in a blended environment at Lakeview High School. As a database instructor for the Library of Michigan, I also now deliver professional development trainings using the online format. While engaged in these projects, I've acquired experience in several online course delivery systems and have embraced a variety of innovative Web 2.0 and social networking tools that barely existed when I was a student at UNT!

The State of Michigan passed landmark legislation in 2006, requiring an approved 20-hour online learning experience for all high school graduates beginning with the Class of 2011. This mandate and my belief that school librarians could play a pivotal role in facilitating online learning at the secondary school level prompted the development of a hybrid online information literacy course at Lakeview High School.

Through conference presentations and journal articles, I have made an effort to share the Lakeview venture into online learning with other school library media professionals who may be involved in similar projects. This opportunity to collaborate with colleagues Dr. Susan Alman and Dr. Christinger Tomer on this publication has allowed me to undertake a more in-depth look at the current status of school libraries and online learning and to make available the information literacy curriculum. The Lakeview experience is one that can be replicated and adapted by other school librarians.

Technological advances are propelling us into an exciting but unknown world. As education moves more and more into a virtual realm, I am convinced that the role of school libraries is certain to evolve so as to continue to support meaningful teaching and learning.

—Margaret Lincoln

Introduction

Sue Alman

A favorite story passed down by library and information science faculty who retired from the University of Pittsburgh in the last millennium involves an inebriated airplane pilot, a snowstorm, and an instructor teaching a library class at a regional campus. The possibly apocryphal tale chronicles the university's first attempt at distance education in the 1970s, when a library and information science faculty member was sent from the main campus in a small chartered airplane to teach a course at one of the university's other campuses. The pilot would wait during class sessions and then fly the instructor back to Pittsburgh. During one winter class session, the pilot passed his time in a local bar while the snow fell steadily. When the instructor boarded the plane after class, it became clear that the pilot was not functioning at the level of precision needed for the return flight. The transportation of faculty to regional campuses did not survive beyond that winter term!

Since that time, the involvement of library and information science faculty in distance education has taken a number of different twists and turns. There are substantiated records of course offerings at the Chautauqua Institution and interactive television courses between students at the main campus and students in other institutions through the 1990s.

The most recent chapter of the story begins in 2000, when the library and information science faculty agreed "in principle" to develop a proposal offering the MLIS program online. This departure from teaching in a traditional classroom was made in response to a growing demand from alumni and prospective students. Individual courses had been offered online at the University of Pittsburgh using Blackboard as the course management system, but the proposal developed for the MLIS program was the first time that a complete degree would be offered asynchronously at the university.

Trial by fire is a powerful learning tool, but we stayed the course and worked hard to create a meaningful academic and social experience for our "pioneer" cohort and the other cohorts that followed them in the past 10 years. The faculty members who proposed and developed the first suite of online courses were on a steep learning curve to understand the philosophy and technology of online education. The group was largely self-taught but gained considerable guidance from a mentor, Dr. Eugene Rubin, University of Maryland University College, who bumped into them quite serendipitously. The MLIS program's current cohort-based educational system is a result of Dr. Rubin's advice.

The FastTrack MLIS Program at the University of Pittsburgh was designed for the busy working adult who is seeking a graduate degree in library and information science but is unable to attend on-campus class sessions. The curriculum and instruction are always the same for students, whether they are on campus or online. The delivery mechanism is the off-setting factor. Registration is on a part-time basis so that students can enroll in two courses each term and complete the degree in six terms, or two calendar years. The first cohorts were introduced to an asynchronous environment that afforded them a weekly PPT and electronic bulletin board chat sessions. As a cohort, they developed back-channel communication techniques and met together once each term in a required on-campus visit.

New technologies were introduced as they became available. Today's online student has access to the university library system's wealth of digital resources, social media, synchronous video broadcasts of on-campus class sessions, and video and audio recordings that capture the classroom activities, in addition to the required on-campus meeting each term.

The FastTrack MLIS Program attracted the attention of two organizations that were seeking graduate library and information science education programs for their constituent groups. As a result, we partnered with the University of the Virgin Islands and the Free Library of Philadelphia and were awarded two IMLS grants to offer the program to their niche audiences. Students from across the United States and Canada and throughout the world have graduated with the MLIS degree. Our FastTrack MLIS alumni have secured positions in all types of libraries and archives, from a small rural public library in Montana to an Ivy League academic library to a multinational corporate library.

The online learning experience is unfamiliar to many instructors and students who have only been exposed to traditional classroom education. An instructor faced with developing and implementing an online learning module, a complete online course, or an entire online program will benefit from reading this compilation of our colleagues' best practices. The chapters in this primer have been written by online education experts who assist us in all aspects of our online program. The advice offered therein will assist the novice and provide suggestions to the seasoned online instructor. We all want to share our experiences with the reader as a way of repaying those who helped us become familiar with the terminology, technology, and techniques of online education.

I

Instructional Design Basics

Barbara A. Frey

INSTRUCTIONAL DESIGN BASICS

Each year, online learning plays an increasingly important role in all fields of education and training. In higher education, a 2010 study by the Sloan Consortium (Allen and Seaman) found that enrollments in online courses grew from 1.6 million students in 2002 to 4.6 million in 2008. The growth rate is 21 percent in online education compared to less than 2 percent growth in overall higher education enrollments. In a similar study for K–12 education, the Sloan Consortium (Anthony and Seaman 2009) reported a substantial 47 percent increase in enrollments in two academic years from 2005/2006 to 2007/2008. It is difficult to measure K–12 enrollments because school districts, state virtual schools, and charter schools report online education in different formats. States such as Florida, Michigan, Pennsylvania, and Alabama have undertaken major initiatives that have had a significant impact on enrollments.

Internet and library resources are a critical component of any distance education curriculum. Information literacy, or the ability to effectively locate, evaluate, and use information, is a core competency for all levels of education. "Information literacy provides a set of skills for sophisticated thinkers who want to use information effectively, not only in an academic setting, but throughout their lives" (Dewald, Crane, Booth, and Levine 2000, 33). Whether planning a web-based stand-alone tutorial on copyright guidelines or a synchronous demonstration on APA style, many librarians lack experience in designing instructional materials for the relatively new medium of online courses. The purpose of this chapter is to summarize the phases of instructional design and provide recommendations for librarian educators who are facilitating online programs and courses.

INSTRUCTIONAL DESIGN MODELS

Instructional design (ID) is part art and part science. Dozens of ID models have been created and studied to help educators develop effective learning experiences with concrete frameworks that guide developers through the decision-making steps. Based on cognitive science, the process is flexible and iterative with interdependence among the steps. To create interesting, engaging, and appealing learning material based on the desired learning outcome requires the instructor and/or designer to incorporate expertise and creativity into the program. Perhaps the three most well-known design models are (1) Dick, Carey, and Carey (2005); (2) Morrison, Ross, and Kemp (2007); and (3) Seels and Glasgow (1990). See Table 1.1 for a summary of these three models.

An analysis of ID models results in a generic, five-phase approach that will be used for our purposes of designing instructional library sessions. The five key

Table 1.1.

Summary of three seminal instructional design models providing systematic project-management processes for developing instruction

Dick, Carey, and Carey (2005)	Morrison, Ross, and Kemp (2007)	Seels and Glasgow (1990)

1. Identify instructional goal(s).
 2. Conduct instructional analysis.
 3. Analyze learners and contexts.
 4. Write performance objectives.
 5. Develop assessment instruments.
 6. Develop instructional strategy.
 7. Develop and select instructional materials.
 8. Design and conduct formative evaluation of instruction.
 9. Revise instruction.
 10. Design and conduct summative evaluation.
	1. Identify instructional problems and specify goals for designing an instructional program.
	 2. Examine learner characteristics that should receive attention during planning.
	 3. Identify subject content and analyze task components related to stated goals and purposes.
	 4. State instructional objectives for the learner.
	 5. Sequence content within each instructional unit for logical learning.
	 6. Design instructional strategies so that each learner can master the objectives.
	 7. Plan the instructional message and delivery.
	 8. Develop evaluation instruments to assess objectives.
	 9. Select resources to support instruction and learning activities.
		1. Phase One: Needs Analysis Management
		   a. goals
		   b. requirements
		   c. context
		 2. Phase Two: Instructional Design Management
		   a. task analysis
		   b. instructional analysis
		   c. objectives and tests
		   d. formative evaluation
		   e. materials development
		   f. instructional strategy and delivery systems
		 3. Phase Three: Implementation Management
		   a. development and production of materials
		   b. delivery of the training
		   c. summative evaluation

phases known as the ADDIE model include (1) analysis, (2) design, (3) development, (4) implementation, and (5) evaluation. This five-step ID model can be used for any level of education or training. Regardless of whether you are planning a traditional face-to-face or an online distance education program, the phases of design are the same; however, the considerations within each phase are different with an online learning environment.

1. Analysis

Many instructors are so eager to teach an online course that they dive into the development before analyzing the necessary components of instruction. For many educators, online learning is a new medium that allows them to try new approaches to teaching and learning. In addition to the convenience and flexibility of online courses, one key difference between traditional face-to-face and online environments is that online students work independently and control their pace and participation in the learning environment. Their work is completed in isolation, but all students have an equal opportunity to ask questions and contribute to discussions. Students posting comments in asynchronous learning programs have time to develop thoughtful responses, and many students value the increased opportunity to interact with their classmates and instructor because there are no time constraints as in traditional on-campus classes. Key questions to consider in the analysis stage are:

- What is the purpose or desired outcome of the program?
- Who are the learners?
- What technology will be used to deliver the learning program?

For our purposes, instructional analysis is divided into three components: analysis of the instructional material, analysis of the students, and analysis of the technology. The analysis of the instructional material begins with the goal or purpose of the program or course within the overall curriculum. Many of the goals and objectives for online courses are converted from face-to-face courses. Online programs can be categorized as foundation, analysis/synthesis, and skills-based courses (Fuller, Kuhne, and Frey 2011). Foundation courses focus on basic introductory material and likely require memorization of core concepts. Analysis/synthesis courses teach higher-level critical thinking or problem-solving skills. Skills-based courses combine cognitive understanding with physical or psychomotor skills such as how to use a computer or specific software. The category of the course will determine the types of activities and assessments.

The more you can discover by analyzing your students, the more effectively you can design their learning experiences. High school students who participate in online courses are likely to be highly literate, independent, motivated, self-disciplined, and technically proficient (Kirby, Sharpe, Bourgeois, and Greene 2010), In higher education, distance education learners are typically older (nontraditional), female, employed full-time, married, highly motivated, self-directed, and autonomous learners (Dewald et al. 2000; Kirby et al. 2010).

The age of your students will contribute to their learning preferences, but it is more important to understand that each individual enrolled in your course is affected by many factors. An instructor can't assume that Jennie, a traditional-age student who is accomplished at multitasking and using her mobile devices, only learns through advanced technologies and multimedia. Much has been written in the literature about "digital natives" who grew up using technology (Prensky 2001), but many adult learners are more adept at using social networking and other web-based technologies than their younger counterparts (Kearns and Frey 2010). Adults value technology tools that allow them to manage their busy lives more effectively.

An analysis of the technology is necessary because of the many types of instructional technologies available for online courses. When motion pictures were first introduced, the new medium was used to simply record stage performances. It was years before movies took full advantage of this new medium. In a similar vein, the delivery of online instructional material requires instructors to analyze their material for this new delivery format. Simply moving materials from face-to-face sessions to static web pages compromises the benefits of the web for dynamic, interactive, nonlinear instruction. In other words, facilitators will want to consider how student interaction with the computer can be more than scrolling through long pages of text.

Delivering an interactive online course can be completed with minimal technological hardware and software using a bare-bones budget, but you can also use a variety of sophisticated technologies that come with hefty price tags. Most courses or presentations are offered within an institutional software system (e.g., Blackboard, Angel, Moodle, and eCollege) that has learning management tools such as discussion forums, blogs, wikis, and a gradebook. An analysis of the available technology tools and applications is critical at the beginning of the design process to know what hardware and software you have at your disposal. In addition to the technology tools, consider the support services offered to you throughout the development and teaching of your course. You may be more comfortable trying advanced technologies to help you achieve your goals if there is support staff to provide training and answer questions.

2. Design

The design phase requires you to identify your final results or outcomes and then work backwards to outline the instructional plan or blueprint that will lead students to achieve those outcomes. The instructional plan includes an outline with the learning objectives, major topics, learning activities, and assessment techniques. In the design phase, developers address the following issues:

- In light of the learning outcomes, what key knowledge and skills should be addressed? In what sequence?
- What activities and instructional media will support learning?
- How will students demonstrate mastery of the learning outcomes?

The objectives or outcomes that you identify for a course will help you stay focused on key components of the instructional program. Wiggins and McTighe (1998) noted that students perform more effectively when they know the desired goal. Bloom's Taxonomy (see Additional Resources at the end of the chapter) is a structured hierarchy of verbs for establishing specific and measureable objectives. These verbs will also distinguish between the lower levels (e.g., list, define, and describe) and higher levels (e.g., apply, analyze, and critique) of thinking required to achieve the outcome. Use the objectives to guide the course materials, activities, discussion topics, and assessments. See Table 1.2 for examples of alignment among learning objectives, activities, and assessments.

Table 1.2.
Alignment between instructional objectives, activities, and assessments

Learning Program	Objectives or Outcomes	Student Activities	Assessments
Librarian facilitating one-module asynchronous workshop on evaluating the credibility of websites for cyber school biology course	Students will be able to: –List criteria to measure credibility of Internet websites –Apply credibility criteria to Internet websites and resources	–Complete online third-party tutorial. –Brainstorm a list of criteria for evaluating websites. –Practice applying a checklist of evaluation criteria to websites.	–Complete true/false or multiple choice quiz. –Respond to essay question assessing websites. –Assess references used in an end-of-term paper.
Embedded librarian in graduate level education course, facilitating synchronous or real-time instruction on American Psychology Association (APA) format	Students will be able to: –Apply APA format to references and literature review paper	–Complete online third-party tutorial. –Identify and use credible Web resources for APA format. –Post APA questions in a discussion forum monitored by a librarian.	–Complete multiple choice or short answer quiz. –Assess references used in an end-of-term paper.

While assessment is addressed at the end of an instructional program in the evaluation phase, best practice in ID calls for early planning with several forms of authentic assessment incorporated throughout the learning program. In some cases, you may want to administer a pretest to determine the students' prior knowledge before teaching your session. Some designers even create their exams prior to developing their learning materials. Effective assessments are beneficial to students and instructors because the feedback allows them to improve their teaching and learning strategies.

3. Development

In the development phase, plans and visions are transformed into concrete materials presented in a clear and logical manner. Development is often the most time-consuming part of the ID process. In this phase, key considerations include:

• To achieve the learning outcomes, what materials should be created for the learning program?
• What visual organizers (e.g., charts, images, graphs) support the learning objectives?
• Will students know the learning goals or outcomes, why the material is important, and what is expected of them?

Online programs can range from one-time workshops to multilesson courses. Courses are usually divided into weekly modules containing an overview, outcomes, reading, lecture, activity or discussion, assignment, and conclusion (See Figure 1.1). In general, the instructor will develop the learning content, but there are also many publisher-created materials and reusable learning objectives (e.g., MERLOT,

Online Course Design

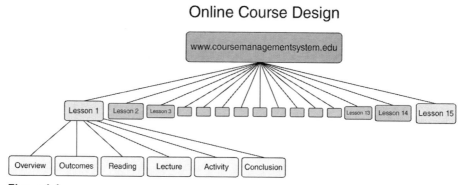

Figure 1.1.
Course development chart organized with weekly modules and components of each module.

Wisc-Online, Maricopa Learning eXchange) that have the potential of saving a lot of development time. Instructor-created presentations can be text based, but there are also more advanced lecture capture technology tools, including narrated slides, screen captures, video, and web-conferencing systems.

Active learning, or engaging students, has a long history with a positive impact on student achievement. Chickering and Ehrman (1999) developed Seven Principles of Good Practice adapted for technology, which include active learning as one of the key principles to effective teaching and learning. Active learning has been linked to student confidence in their knowledge, retention of concepts, learning motivation, and problem-solving skills (Bakke and Faley 2007). Online education offers numerous opportunities for diverse and interactive forms of learning such as group work, role play, discussion forums, online exercises, practice quizzes, simulations, and presentations. Recommendations for active learning include having a clear purpose, establishing a definite beginning and ending, providing clear instructions and expectations, and offering some form of feedback (Mantyla 1999).

Students taking online courses do not have the advantage of being able to see your facial expressions or other visual cues; therefore, you will want to be very clear and specific in your words and expectations. Strive for a friendly, informal writing style with concise sentences and paragraphs balanced with plenty of white space. Clearly organize instructional materials with headings and subheadings and emphasize key text with bold or italicized words. Avoid underlining that makes the text look like a hyperlink or colored text that may be difficult for color-blind or vision-impaired students to read. Select a font, such as Verdana or Georgia, that is designed for reading on a computer screen.

4. Implementation

During implementation, the teaching librarian puts the instructional plan into action. Some general questions addressed during the implementation phase of ID include:

• What is the learner's reaction to each component of the instructional program?
• What are the forms of interaction with the content, learners, and instructor?

- Is the overall program coherent and effective?
- To what degree are the activities appropriate and manageable?

For both the instructor and the student, online teaching and learning require different skills from those of face-to-face teaching and learning. Ideally, you and your students will have prepared for the online environment with an orientation to the distance learning tools. Offering the first implementation of the program as a small-scale pilot study will allow you to test the process and make modifications. A small pilot study will also allow you to measure the time that it takes to complete various activities in the course. Participating in online discussions, quizzes, and exercises takes longer in an online course than it does in an on-campus course. Monitoring and adjusting the workload will prevent you and your students from becoming overwhelmed with course tasks.

5. Evaluation

For our purposes, there are two types of evaluation: evaluation of student learning and evaluation of the effectiveness of the course. Following are key considerations in the evaluation phase of instructional design:

- What is the level of student learning? Is it acceptable?
- To what degree are objectives achieved?
- What revisions are necessary to the content, activities, and/or assessments?

Evaluation of student learning includes formative (ongoing evaluations) and summative (final evaluations) assessments that allow facilitators to monitor student progress and make program modifications. The purpose of formative evaluation is to identify ways of strengthening a course while it is being taught. Formative evaluation, present in every phase of the instructional process, may be practice quizzes, journals, discussion questions, or observations of students' reactions. The purpose of summative evaluation is to assess the final overall value of the program and ways to improve it. Summative evaluation often includes reviews of final exams, term papers, portfolios, or major projects.

The program learning objectives or outcomes indicate the types of assessment that will measure student learning and performance. If the objective states a high-level verb according to Bloom's Taxonomy, such as "analyze key descriptors and Boolean logic in a database search," the assessment might be a case study ending with analysis-level multiple choice items or essay questions. Your instructional session or course will likely be modified after reviewing the results of student performance on the assessments. Student errors will indicate weaknesses or areas of confusion in the instructional program.

Evaluating the effectiveness of the course or session is especially important because you do not see the physical reactions of your students. Many new instructors administer both midpoint and end-of-program evaluation surveys. The anonymous survey questions should assess student reactions to the course materials, delivery format, teacher, activities, and assignments (Dewald et al. 2000). Student feedback can be a valuable source of information used to improve the course.

INSTRUCTIONAL DESIGN EXAMPLE USING ADDIE MODEL

Victoria West-Pawl, MLIS, from Colorado State University's Global Campus (CSU Global) provides online library instruction and support to approximately 3,500 undergraduate and graduate students. Prior to developing any instructional programs, she asked both faculty and students about their problem areas and recommendations for library sessions or tutorials. Students were having trouble citing in APA, writing research papers, and finding resources in the library. One of the first tutorials that Victoria created, "Finding Resources in the Library" (See Figure 1.2), applied the following ADDIE instructional design model:

I. Analysis

Victoria approaches the design of instructional programs by putting herself in the role of the student who may be overwhelmed with responsibilities, nervous about online learning, and unfamiliar with instructional technology. Most CSU Global students are returning to college after years of work and life experiences. With a median age of 36, they may have little experience using digital collections or databases.

From informal interviews with faculty, Victoria discovered that one of the challenges that faculty face is students who use the Internet for research rather than the more credible and scholarly references of the academic library. The more assertive students often requested individualized support through the library search process, but the majority of students were unaware of the support that Victoria provided.

2. Design

"Finding Resources in the Library" is presented as a 30- to 45-minute synchronous session offered several times during the first few weeks of each term. The instructional session is not required, but some instructors give extra credit for participating, which has increased student attendance. Victoria facilitates the introductory session with the Wimba web-conferencing system and archives the files for on-demand viewing at students' convenience.

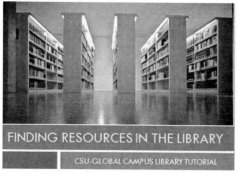

Figure I.2.
CSU-Global tutorial "Finding Resources in the Library."
(used with permission)

The overall goal for the session is to familiarize students with the library resources. More specifically, the objectives are based on the Association of College and Research Libraries (ACRL) information literacy standards:

1. Determine the extent of information needed
2. Access the needed information effectively and efficiently
3. Evaluate information and its sources critically
4. Use information effectively to accomplish a specific purpose
5. Understand the economic, legal, and social issues surrounding the use of information, and access and use information ethically and legally

3. Development

The Wimba session begins with a virtual tour of the library resources and then step-by-step instructions for searching databases and locating resources. Victoria also integrates the ACRL information literacy standards into her sessions. Working closely with faculty and reviewing many of the course assignments helps Victoria to incorporate specific information about the various student projects into her sessions. Since "Finding Resources in the Library" is an introductory session, there are often follow-up questions regarding specific course assignments. Students can contact the library through instant messaging, text messaging, telephone, e-mail, or chat.

4. Implementation

Victoria notes that one of the challenges of online teaching is that she does not see her students' facial expressions or reactions; therefore, she is not instantly sure if they understand her presentation. She strives to get students involved as soon as possible by asking questions that require a student response (e.g., Who has used Wimba? Does anyone want to share a topic they are working on? Has anyone heard of the information literacy standards?). Another presentation strategy is pausing after a few slides so students have the opportunity to ask questions.

5. Evaluation

The "Finding Resources in the Library" session ends with five feedback questions for student participants:

- Did you find this session to be useful?
- What did you find to be the most useful?
- Are there any areas to improve this session?
- What times are best for you to take an open session?
- What other open session would you like to see offered?

Like every instructional design project, "Finding Resources in the Library" is in a constant state of revision. The session design, content, and delivery are tweaked every term, integrating both student and faculty feedback. Victoria is a regular presenter and attendee at the online faculty meetings, which opens channels for ongoing communication with the instructors. Faculty members consider Victoria to be a critical contributor to the teaching mission of the university.

CONCLUSION

Online learning is a relatively new format for delivering instructional programs. It offers the opportunity to provide meaningful learning experiences, diverse instructional materials, and engaging activities that are accessible by students at any time and from any place. Library and information literacy instruction is a critical component of any online program. The explosion of information and the short shelf life of knowledge require students in every discipline to develop skills for lifelong learning.

Many teaching librarians use instructional design models such as the ADDIE framework (analysis, design, development, implementation, and evaluation) to systematically plan and organize high-quality programs. The arrangement of resources and procedures has a major impact on student learning. Instructional design provides a logical process for transforming *information* into student-centered *instruction* by developing learning activities and assessments based on the goals or desired outcomes of the learning program or session. Course development is an ongoing, iterative process that incorporates feedback and evaluation to continually improve the course content and delivery.

FURTHER READING

Bloom's Taxonomy from Old Dominion University (http://www.odu.edu/educ/roverbau/Bloom/blooms_taxonomy.htm)
In 1956, Benjamin Bloom led a group of educational psychologists to develop six classifications for cognitive learning objectives. The lists of verbs associated with each category help educators develop specific, measureable, and observable learning objectives for their students.

Carnegie Mellon Open Learning Initiative (http://www.cmu.edu/oli) and Massachusetts Institute of Technology Open Courseware (http://ocw.mit.edu/index.htm)
It is immensely helpful to review examples of online courses, but most courses are within password-protected websites. Two open initiatives that provide numerous examples are MIT's Open Courseware and CMU's Open Learning Initiative.

eLearning Guide (http://liad.georgebrown.ca/liadhome/e-learning%20guide/index.html)
George Brown College in Canada offers an extensive e-Learning Guide with suggestions and templates for planning and developing online courses.

Illinois Online Network (http://www.ion.uillinois.edu/resources/tutorials/id/index.asp)
The University of Illinois initiative Illinois Online Network supports online education with numerous faculty development courses and resources.

Index of Learning Styles Questionnaire by Barbara A. Soloman and Richard M. Felder at North Carolina State University (http://www.engr.ncsu.edu/learningstyles/ilsweb.html)
The electronic questionnaire assesses a user's learning style to determine whether it is active or reflective, sensing or intuitive, visual or verbal, and sequential or global.

Online course syllabus template from California State University, Sacramento (www.csus.edu/atcs/tools/instructional/templates/syllabus/t-online-syllabus.doc)
This template provides an accessible, organized document for building your course syllabus.

Quality Matters (http://www.qmprogram.org)

Quality Matters (QM) is a nonprofit organization that offers a faculty-centered peer review process to certify the quality of online courses. Both K–12 and postsecondary institutions subscribe to the QM course review services and training materials.

REFERENCES

Allen, I. Elaine, and Jeff Seaman. 2010. "Class Differences: Online Education in the United States, 2010." Babson Survey Research Group and The Sloan Consortium. November 2010. Accessed June 1, 2011. http://sloanconsortium.org/publications/survey/pdf/class_differences.

Bakke, Sharen, and Robert H. Faley. 2007. "A Student-centric Approach to Large Introductory IS Survey Courses." *Journal of Information Systems Education* 18 (3): 321–28.

Chickering, Arthur W., and Steve C. Ehrman. 1996. "Implementing the Seven Principles: Technology as a Lever." *American Association for Higher Education Bulletin* 10: 3–6.

Dick, Walter, Lou Carey, and James O. Carey. 2005. *The Systematic Design of Instruction* (6th ed.). Boston: Allyn & Bacon.

Dewald, Nancy, Ann Scholz-Crane, Austin Booth, and Cynthia Levine. 2000. "Information Literacy at a Distance: Instructional Design Issues." *Journal of Academic Librarianship* 26 (1): 33–44.

Fuller, Richard G., Gary W. Kuhne, and Barbara A. Frey. 2011. *Distinctive Distance Education Design: Models for Differentiated Instruction.* New York, NY: Information Science Reference.

Kearns, Lorna R., and Barbara A. Frey. 2010. "Web 2.0 Technologies and Back Channel Communication in an Online Learning Community." *TechTrends* 54 (4): 41–51.

Kirby, Dale, Dennis Sharpe, Monique Bourgeois, and Melanie Greene. 2010. "Graduates of the New Learning Environment: A Follow-Up Study of High School Distance eLearners." *The Quarterly Review of Distance Education* 11 (3): 161–73.

Mantyla, Karen. 1999. *Interactive Distance Learning Exercises That Really Work!* Alexandria, VA: American Society of Training and Development.

Morrison, Gary R., Steven M. Ross, and Jerrold E. Kemp. 2007. *Designing Effective Instruction* (3rd ed.). New York: John Wiley & Sons.

Picciano, Anthony G., and Jeff Seaman. 2009. "K–12 Online Learning: A 2008 Follow-Up of the Survey of U.S. School District Administrators." Babson Survey Group, CUNY: Hunter College and Graduate Center, and The Sloan Consortium. Accessed May 27, 2011. http://sloanconsortium.org/publications/survey/pdf/k-12_online_learning_2008.pdf.

Prensky, Marc. 2001. "Digital Natives, Digital Immigrants." *On the Horizon* 9 (5). Accessed May 30, 2011. http://www.marcprensky.com/writing/Prensky%20-%20Digital%20Natives,%20Digital%20Immigrants%20-%20Part1.pdf.

Seels, Barbara, and Zita Glasgow. 1990. *Exercises in Instructional Technology.* Columbus, OH: Merrill Publishing Co.

Wiggins, Grant, and Jay McTighe. 1998. *Understanding by Design.* Alexandria, VA: Association for Supervision and Curriculum Development.

2

Faculty Development in Online Education

Kelly Otter

INTRODUCTION

Creating and teaching a course through a distance education environment can be a new challenge for many faculty members, and professional development and training for faculty members who teach at a distance is an essential component of successful online programs. Discussions about the differences and contrasting benefits of face-to-face versus online education are often circumscribed by assumptions about the correlation between interaction and learning, and about what kinds of learning environments facilitate interaction. When transitioning from the traditional classroom to the online environment, instructors often privilege the former modality as one that must be replicated in a learning management system (LMS) to ensure that the attributes of effective teaching and learning will be present. They often seek to reproduce lecture and assignment material and model online discussions on classroom discussions, with the hope of invoking a similar, if not identical, level of learning in students.

Once teachers are immersed in the online environments, they are often surprised to discover the degree to which the dynamics of teaching and learning have shifted, and to realize how many choices they must make in the process of designing their courses to optimize the opportunity to achieve expected outcomes. Finally, teachers are often unaware of the extent to which the institution hosting the online course or program has or will invest resources in an infrastructure to support quality online instruction. What will follow in this chapter is a discussion of some primary areas for faculty to consider as they prepare to teach online: the requirements of the instructor to teach online; the process of transitioning to the new modality; and questions teachers should be prepared to ask about the operational, student, and faculty support provided by the institutions for which they teach.

TEACHING ONLINE

Instructors have a myriad of ways to teach online. New online instructors should consider their own attributes as teachers, the nature of their learning audiences, the needs of the discipline, and their interest in engaging with various types of technology on a frequent basis before determining course structure. Online instructors must develop specialized skills and strategies, especially with careful course planning, organization, and being prepared to communicate with learners in new ways.

Teachers should consider whether they prefer to teach exclusively in the online environment, or if the course requires a face-to-face component. Some people are dynamic in the classroom but not in the online environment, and vice versa. Social media tools are good for teachers who thrive on face-to-face interaction, and discussion boards serve the asynchronous format by allowing students to carefully craft their written responses and read the teacher's and other students' comments at their convenience.

The general perception is that a considerable time commitment is required of instructors in any form of online modality, as the design process and teaching are generally more labor-intensive than for traditional classroom instruction. The frequent inclusion of written explanations and discussion tools creates a heavy amount of reading and writing, and the fact that class time extends beyond the boundaries of a defined place and time can lead to multiple interactions with students on a weekly, or even daily, basis. Because of the absence of a contiguous and synchronous experience, instructors often feel the need to engage with students by responding to most, if not all, discussion board posts and e-mail messages. In a sense, class is always in session and the instructor is never off the clock. Moreover, unlike previous decades when classes met one or two times a week, an instructor held office hours, and the only communication tools were letters, notes, and telephones, students in the electronic communication era have been oriented to social interaction with devices (e-mail, text, social media) that allow for immediate responses. Students often expect e-mail responses from instructors the same day they are sent, if not immediately. Instructors should define the amount and frequency of interaction so that they are accessible to students, but in a manner that is predictable and well-structured for both the teacher and students. Also, students can work in teams when appropriate, and the instructor can play the role of facilitator or mentor in their interactions with groups of learners rather than communicating only on an individual basis.

In the web environment, the best approach is to think about the course development as a transformation of what you normally do rather than re-creating the content of a classroom course. You will find you must "rethink" both learning activities and objectives within the context of the web environment, and this includes adding resources and dealing with new limitations.

Some personal and professional benefits of teaching online are that it

- provides the opportunity to learn about the fields of instructional design and instructional technology
- provides the opportunity to learn about traditional and online pedagogies
- provides an opportunity to learn about cutting-edge technologies
- connects instructors with a new community of innovative individuals, both in the course development process and by introducing them to a community of instructors who teach online and can share best practices and feedback
- increases an instructor's teaching portfolio, expanding employment opportunities

Most educational institutions provide training on the LMS, such as Blackboard, as well as the services of instructional designers and technologists. However, if these resources are not provided, online course developers will need to become familiar with the components and capabilities of the LMS and assess their own technological expertise and interest in learning new skills. Instructors should be comfortable with these common tasks:

- creating and cutting and pasting documents using word-processing software
- communicating via e-mail
- opening and using web browsers
- creating folders
- creating content and uploading it in a LMS
- creating links to various websites and content on the Internet
- creating voice or visual recordings of content presentation and embedding them in the LMS

Kearsly and Blomeyer provide a good summary of some of the competencies for online instructors that are closely aligned with the National Educational Technology Standards (NETS) as established by International Society for Technology in Education (ISTE):

- Be proficient using the basic elements of online courses: e-mail, threaded discussions, real-time conferencing (chats).
- Be able to describe the characteristics of successful distance learners.
- Be able to describe techniques for effective online teaching.
- Be able to evaluate the quality of online learning programs.
- Be able to explain the ethical and legal issues associated with online education.
- Be able to explain the accessibility issues associated with online education.
- Be able to describe strategies for integrating online and classroom instruction.

Instructors can develop proficiency in various LMS communication tools during the course of the development process, but, as adult learning principles suggest, faculty members need to experience technology and pedagogical strategies firsthand before they begin to teach their classes. An online course or module in instructional design for faculty could be effective for this purpose, as well as to develop awareness of the characteristics of successful students in an online environment. Faculty also benefit from the opportunity to be mentored by an experienced faculty member or technologist to learn to utilize the features of the LMS and learn strategies to efficiently manage the workflow associated with online teaching. Examples of modules include the following:

- LMS module—address the use of the LMS and other computing tools (such as Word and PowerPoint) that can facilitate the creation of web-based course materials
- Instructional design module—build faculty skills and knowledge by examining the connection between the course content and the instructional design process. Topics covered could include understanding the online student audience and the differences in teaching online; creating course learning objectives; designing learning activities that promote active learning; integrating rich media elements such as blogs, video clips, wikis, portfolios, primary source materials, educational games, simulations, and other learning objects into instruction; and creating assessment activities that measure the process and the product of learning.

- Online facilitation module—provide faculty with an understanding of a variety of online learning models. The course will help faculty build their facilitation skills in an online environment. They will also learn how to manage the workload associated with teaching an online course. Topics covered include: changing faculty roles and expectations, building rapport and a sense of community with online students, initiating and facilitating online discussions, taking advantage of all course features and rich media objects, providing feedback to students, and managing workload and faculty expectations issues.

Modules could be conducted asynchronously so faculty members can experience effective online teaching strategies and model those behaviors as they integrate them into their practice. Cohorts allow for the creation of a support network of faculty members as they build their skills.

Techniques for effective online teaching emphasize centering on the learner. Because online courses are more learner centered, they often require more active participation by every student, rather than those who hold up their hands in the traditional classroom. Faculty will no longer be limited to a specific block of time on a certain day of the week, which allows them much more flexibility in the design of all assignments, discussion topics, and other projects. Without the traditional structure of weekly classes, students are generally expected to take a more active role in their own learning, which means working throughout the week rather than preparing before coming to a traditional class. When learners share their ideas with the instructor and other members of the class, everyone acquires and interprets new information, making it more meaningful. Such interactions form the foundation of a community of learners. When students understand that they are a part of their community of learners, they are more likely to be motivated to seek solutions to problems, which helps them succeed. Distance educators must meet the challenge and develop new strategies and techniques to establish and maintain "learning communities" among their students who are separated by space and/or time.

When the learning goals and objectives are identified and articulated, they become the foundation for the instructional design, which is the development, delivery, and assessment of each educational event. The definition of these goals serves as the implied contract between instructors and students and acts as a roadmap of what will be taught and what students are expected to learn. The instructor's adherence to the articulated learning goals becomes a crucial step in ensuring an effective learning experience for students. These learning outcomes are very similar to face-to-face instruction; however, these new instructional design strategies are needed to support the anticipated outcomes stated for the distance learning class.

Assessment and measurement serve many valuable purposes for both distant learning instructors and their students. They give instructors information on the progress of learners and help them measure achievement toward the learning goals. They provide learners with benchmarks for monitoring their progress, thus allowing them to adjust their learning strategies. Online instruction assessment also incorporates measures to gather information not only about student learning but also about course management, design, and delivery. In a distance education model, assessment and measurement become even more critical in the absence of the face-to-face interactions that enable teachers to use informal observation to gauge student response, obtain feedback, and progress toward goals. Creativity in the design and approach to assessment and measurement strategies can serve both the instructor and the learner in the distance education setting. Many universities provide a testing center that offers opportunities for testing students on campus. They may also find proctoring services or off-campus testing sites for students living far from campus. However, online instructors should be encouraged to consider some new ways they may wish to assess their students. These include postings to discussion boards, long-term projects, essays, and other innovative tools for students to use such as blogs and wikis. Quiz functions in the LMS can be very effective, but they give rise to academic integrity issues because instructors cannot monitor whether students complete the quiz independently. Some instructors employ the function as an ungraded exercise to ensure that students have grasped specific concepts or learned an assigned vocabulary. Others use the tool and limit the amount of time the quiz is available so that only students who know the material well will be able to complete the task in the allotted amount of time.

Evaluation instruments and methods should closely align with best practices for online evaluation, and information gathered from evaluations should be used to refine course materials and plan faculty professional development opportunities. Formative (while the course is in progress) and summative (after the course is complete) evaluation instruments provide teachers feedback that can be incorporated during the course to improve the learning experience, and when the course is complete so that modifications can be made before the course is offered again.

Faculty must be aware of their institutions' requirements to comply with federal regulations, especially those associated with the Americans with Disabilities Act. Course design must take into consideration how to construct content so that it is accessible to students with sight or hearing impairments. Instructors should employ screen readers and voice-recognition software if the institution can provide them. One of the values of course management systems is that they offer closed and password-protected networks and closed access to all activities, discussions, and assignments, which are only accessible to the instructor and the students enrolled in the course or to administrators, technical support personnel, and help desk administrators who are responsible for maintaining access to all sites within the institution.

Intellectual property laws are continuously under review with regard to digitized materials, and questions about fair use are frequently raised, so there is no single set of guidelines to follow that takes into account all the possible ways to incorporate digitized content (journal articles, photographs, video, cartoons, images) in an online course.

It is important to gather and/or locate other resources, including readings, media, additional websites, and images, as you plan your course. Instructors must be prepared to let students know of any technology requirements. If a high-speed connection or the ability to download iTunes or other special configurations are needed, students should be made aware at the beginning of each class. Also, provide information to students at the outset about what browsers are compatible with the LMS and the various types of tools and media that are incorporated into your course. G. Salmon says that students will likely be unfamiliar with the software tools you choose to use, and it is important to show them how to use these tools while they *are taking part in online e-tivities* that are interesting and relevant to them." Students will arrive with a range of experiences with technology: most adults use electronic communication tools in the workplace, and many K–12 students are highly skilled with video games and massively multiplayer online role-playing games (MMORPGs); thus, age and gender are not reliable for predicting level or type of experience with technology.

The best strategies for integrating classroom and online instruction can be explored in consultation with instructional designers to determine the correct mix of instructional methods based on the course objectives. Schmidt and Brown present a useful model for integrating online teaching strategies into the classroom that emphasizes the dynamic and iterative process of integrating technology and classroom instruction. They discuss the following steps:

- Examine your teaching style.
- Assess your students' preferred learning styles.
- Study online and traditional teaching and learning tools.
- Select online teaching and learning tools.
- Reflect, implement, reflect, revise.

Students will do many of the same things in the online environment that they would do if they were in a more traditional classroom, such as reading texts, taking notes, answering questions, writing papers, and having discussions. They may also be assigned to use specified computer software, to watch videos, and to conduct field observations. The difference between their online experience and a more traditional one is that most often all interaction takes place in their web environment.

Further, while technology allows for multiple interactions that allow for the building of knowledge through feedback and written dialogue, it also facilitates and enables a more dynamic environment that allows for new teaching and learning strategies to emerge.

Because this model is dynamic, it is expected that teachers will need to be open to continuous change. Students' learning styles may vary widely from student to student, new online teaching and learning tools will continue to be developed, and an increased awareness of one's teaching style will lead to modifications within the composition of online tools and classroom interaction.

(Schmidt and Brown 89)

As faculty consider the professional and pedagogical opportunities in the process of teaching online, it is also important that they consider the perspective of the student, for whom there are also numerous benefits. Just a few of them include:

- access to high-quality educational experiences for those who might not have otherwise had the learning opportunity due to geographic or time constraints
- access to resources that can be viewed and studied 24 hours a day, 7 days a week
- the opportunity to engage with new teaching strategies and to develop and demonstrate new competencies
- technologies and collaborative learning techniques to help them develop skills they will need in the technology-based workplace
- a learning environment that many find more comfortable and less stressful than the classroom

A constructive notion for teachers new to online instruction to consider early in the course design process is the degree to which traditional classroom instruction is founded on the authority of the instructor, whose presentation of material is often performance-based. The guide is positioned to facilitate the construction of knowledge by evoking participation of the learners who comment, critique, and analyze. This engagement with materials and other learners produces a social environment that shares the construction of knowledge, but also foregrounds for the instructor how the students, individually and collectively, comprehend, apply, and communicate the material and concepts. Whereas the sage is often the holder and transmitter of knowledge who assesses the learner via assignments produced in isolation, the guide is better able to transcend the presentation and assessment dyad, and facilitate deeper, more thorough explorations among the learners.

The instructor often stands in the front of the class, literally on a stage, positioned to be viewed and heard by all students simultaneously. The voice is projected, and at times amplified. We could easily view the traditional classroom as a technology that favors certain forms of instruction and reproduces the authority of the instructor by creating the conditions in which students focus primarily on the presence of the instructor. The architecture of the traditional classroom—e.g., the manner in which the chalkboard, screen, and podium cluster around the teacher—creates conditions in which students' attention focuses on the figure of the instructor. Furthermore, the distribution of space reproduces the authority and importance of the instructor. Students do not speak while the instructor is speaking, and they request to be recognized when it is appropriate for them to ask a question or make a comment.

The role of the instructor shifts in technology-mediated modalities from that of an authoritative presenter with expert knowledge to that of an expert whose knowledge is transmitted or channeled through various media: textual, visual, and auditory. The shift in space, time, and channel necessarily changes the interaction. With the lecture as its preferred mode of address, the traditional classroom carries with it a predictable decorum that reliably regulates the conditions of class discussion. However, in online discussions, students often quote from the course readings on their own, with no prompting from the instructor. They also tend to address their questions and concerns to the entire class, not always directly to the instructor. Imagine students in a face-to-face class raising their hands and asking *other students* for assistance in understanding or grasping a concept or term. Students also share and circulate materials that they believe enrich or clarify the topic at hand. Once again, imagine students in a face-to-face classroom passing out an article they found to supplement assigned material, or that they found more accessible or informative than the assigned reading.

MODELS OF COURSE BUILDING AND STAFFING

Numerous variations in the types and structure of online courses address the needs of the teaching style of the instructor, the required capacity of the course, and the available technology and institutional support for development and maintenance. Online courses can be constructed with numerous combinations of material presentation and interactions through reading, writing, listening, watching, and speaking. Models that replicate the lecture format of traditional classroom instruction incorporate live or recorded lectures. Other common models are those in which instructors present written directions, assignments, and activities in the LMS and the class engages via discussion boards as a whole group, or small groups, or on an individual basis with the instructor.

Common types of online courses include the following:

- Online courses—all content and interaction take place in a LMS
- Hybrid courses—content and interaction take place in a LMS, and face-to-face sessions are required
- Self-paced/correspondence

Courses offered exclusively online in a LMS are generally structured so that students interact with instructors and other students through the LMS. They will move through the materials as a cohort, and they usually complete their requirements for the course within one term. All course requirements for reading, discussion, homework, and assessment are conducted online. Hybrid courses combine both mandatory face-to-face instruction and web-based interaction and other activities. Students are required to attend these scheduled meetings or workshops, and they must also participate in all other online activities. For other hybrid models, students attend face-to-face meetings only for the first and/or the last session of their course; still others require meetings assigned throughout the entire term. These meetings are held for various activities that require in-person inter-action such as group projects, presentations, or viewing a class report. Students in this configuration also proceed through the materials as a cohort, and they are expected to complete all course requirements within one term. While both purely online and hybrid courses can allow for students to complete assignments at their convenience, these courses generally have a solid structure with deadlines at regular intervals.

Self-paced or correspondence courses, which incorporate many of the features described above, also provide a flexible format for students to work through their assigned course materials at their own pace. While workshops and web-based activities are offered in many of these courses, and even though they are well structured and usually have clear study guides, this flexibility means that students must be highly self-motivated and be able to manage their time well. Self-paced courses incorporate a variety of delivery methods, including workshops, textbooks, print study guides, and online communication. The courses are designed so interaction occurs at workshops and via telephone, mail, and e-mail. Many of the courses have an online component, but the self-paced nature of the courses limits opportunities for extended interaction between faculty and students. Com-parative studies of students enrolled in self-paced and cohort-based online courses at the College of General Studies, University of Pittsburgh, have shown that completion rates in the self-paced model are significantly lower when students are not required to adhere to a well-defined assignment schedule and deadlines.

Common tools that can be used to deliver content in a traditional lecture format can be incorporated in any of the models described above. A few include the following:

- Web or video conferencing in a LMS can be synchronous or asynchronous. Video conferencing allows for asynchronous meeting between parties in different locations, though each location must have the same specialized equipment. Webcasting only requires the sending location to have the equipment, while the viewer needs only a web browser and an Internet connection.
- Voice over Internet Protocol (VoIP) allows for voice calls to be made over the Internet and for parties at different locations to see images of each other in real time.
- Podcasts and MP3 or video files can be downloaded and played on a computer or portable device.

Online, hybrid, self-paced courses require the instructor to consider the nature of the discipline, materials, and activities and the degree to which technology will allow students to effectively engage with the content or activity. Some tools available through most LMS systems include the following:

- discussion boards (asynchronous)
- chat sessions (synchronous)
- assignments feature
- virtual classroom or group pages
- PowerPoint presentations
- wikis
- blogs

THE TRANSITION FROM FACE-TO-FACE TO ONLINE

Typically, a course development project can require three months to one year; however, the time necessary will vary by the competency of the faculty member in designing online instruction and by the academic discipline of the course. Faculty developers benefit from meeting with an instructional designer to establish a timeline that will include benchmarks for completion and expectations for development. It can also be helpful to participate in Sloan Consortium online workshops and develop a network of faculty peers who teach online. Faculty members who are new to online course development are often unfamiliar with the work of instructional designers; conversely, instructional designers often face the challenge of overcoming unfamiliarity with the discipline of the course being designed. Differences of opinion and approach will arise. No rule can determine the best choice when these differences occur, but they usually arise from a lack of experience or understanding of one or the other field. The designer/technologist must understand the goals of the instructor for employing technology in the teaching process. If the designer is not also a technologist, a team approach that includes a technologist will be beneficial.

In the first meeting with an instructional designer/technologist, it is helpful for teachers to review and become familiar with course templates from a variety of disciplines that employ synchronous and asynchronous tools. It will also be helpful for the designer to learn about the strategies employed by the instructor in the face-to-face environment; he or she should be prepared to discuss some technological tools that replicate or improve on those strategies.

- Review examples of how video conferencing, webcasting, and VoIP tools such as Skype, are used. Ask whether your institution owns any of these tools or whether it is willing to purchase them. If not, consider open-source options and whether your technological skill level will allow you to use them effectively.
- Review samples of discussion board and chat sessions for a variety of models used with a range of class sizes.
- Review examples of media-rich courses, especially those that use web-based resources and visual materials, and determine the technical requirements necessary for students using personal computers.
- Review features in the LMS that will facilitate student learning activities or be appropriate for content presentation and discussions.

The rubric below was developed by the College of General Studies at the University of Pittsburgh[1] to guide faculty through the process of transitioning from traditional classroom courses or text-based distance education courses to highly interactive online courses. A distinction is made between static and dynamic elements: those that provide information or content without interaction from the instructor or another class member, as opposed to those elements in that stimulate engagement. Faculty use the rubric in the design process, and it is incorporated into the approval process. A minimum number of required static and dynamic features must be built into each course to meet the program standards for interactivity.

Interactivity Rubric

N	Interaction Category	Type	Description/Examples/ Notes	Potential BB/Cour- seweb/Other Gools	Minimum
1	student-to-student	static	A single introduction posting made by the student.	discussion board, blog, wiki, student homepage	1
2		dynamic	The goal could be for them to learn from each other (exchange or debate) or to collaborate (group project).	discussion board, chat, virtual classroom (e.g., WebEx), group file exchange, blog, wiki, digital drop box	1
3	instructor-to-student	dynamic	Non-prepackaged interactions that are situation-dependent and responsive to the student.	discussion board, chat, virtual classroom (e.g., WebEx), group file exchange, blog, wiki, digital drop box	1 (diff. type)
4	instructor-to-student student-to-materials	static	Presentations, readings, articles, audio presentations, assigned readings.	content items, blog, wiki, audio/video uploads, attachments, glossary	some variety
5	student-to-materials	dynamic	Materials that respond to learner's input.	(non-BB tools, usually off-site)	0
6	student-to-instructor	static	A single student response to an instructor's assignment, quiz, or test.	digital drop box, quiz tool, discussion board with restricted access, blog, wiki	2
7			Student-initiated interactions, such as office hours.	virtual classroom (e.g., WebEx)	0

Faculty members have choices to make regarding how to incorporate content into an online learning experience. Two common building models present options that suit a variety of teaching style sand disciplines:

- *Model 1: Faculty-developed materials*—Faculty members develop and design online and hybrid courses in their areas of expertise, either independently or with the support of an instructional designer and/or instructional technologist.
- *Model 2: Faculty-mediated materials*—Faculty members adopt predeveloped course objects and materials in their classes. These materials enable teachers to embed a richer variety of materials into their courses than is possible with traditional "do-it-yourself" learning devices.

In addition, these materials can be customized and combined with faculty-created content to design a rich online learning experience for students. These objects will save faculty members time and allow for quicker development and implementation of courses.

Learning and course objects have been developed by a variety of different groups. A selected source list for learning and course objects includes:

- Open Content Initiative, featuring course content developed by major research institutions such as the Massachusetts Institute of Technology, The Johns Hopkins University, Rice University, and Carnegie Mellon University
- Traditional textbook publishers
- Multimedia instructional developers, e.g., MindEdge
- Course objects produced by the Multimedia Educational Resource for Learning and Online Teaching (MERLOT)

ASSESS THE INSTITUTIONAL INFRASTRUCTURE

Faculty should survey the culture, resources, and infrastructure available at the institution to determine what level of support exists for online and other technology-mediated education. The attitudes about using technology to explore new pedagogies and the provision of access through distance education will have an impact on the resources provided and the quality of the teaching experience. Each institution is unique in its interest in, approaches to, and support for online education, so teachers need to be prepared with an understanding of the culture and context in which they will be teaching. Support services are key when challenges arise that are outside the classroom or technical in nature, because students seek assistance from their instructors, who are never equipped to solve every problem.

A list of questions to consider and research is the following:

(1) Development resources:
- Is one or more LMS available, and is there trained support staff to offer workshops and troubleshoot?
- Are instructional designers and technologists available to assist faculty with the creation of courses, to design features using HTML, to build simulations and other interactive tools, and to integrate tools from publishers' materials that you are incorporating into your course?
- Are technology support staff available to do coding, create images, or assist with video creation and uploading? Is a streaming server available?
- What is the institution's policy on intellectual property rights with regard to materials used in your online course? What, according to your institution, constitutes fair use? Does the library have an electronic reserve service to link to copyrighted materials purchased by the institution? Will the institution acquire copyright clearance, or is this the instructor's responsibility?
- What is the institution's policy on intellectual property rights with regard to materials you create specifically for the course? Do you own the content, does the institution own it, or is it a joint ownership agreement? If you are paid to develop the content, does the institution consider this a work-for-hire arrangement?

(2) Learner Support:
Among the most important components in the design of distance education programs are those that establish the organizational and administrative infrastructures required to ensure

that such programs can be efficiently and effectively developed, managed, and executed. The learner support systems and services required to establish and maintain an effective distance education experience must be at least as complete, as responsive, and as student oriented as those provided for the on-campus learner. Examples include the following:

- Online orientation—a short, self-paced experience designed to help students build the skills and knowledge they need to successfully complete online courses. The program should present course or program expectations, outline available resources, and help students to navigate the new learning experience.
- Enrollment support—provide online application and admission and registration support.
- Financial aid—provide online financial aid services, including entrance and exit counseling.
- Online mentors—Online mentors would contact students prior to the start of the course and would periodically maintain contact with students in selected high-enrollment classes. These mentors would provide assistance and encouragement and assist faculty by answering routine questions and providing support to students.
- Advising—Students should be able to access advising information and services online. Advisors should schedule asynchronous e-mail and real-time chat advising sessions.
- Writing and math support—Students should have electronic access to academic support services such as writing and math tutors, and other support services provided in the disciplines.
- Assessment and testing—Testing should be conducted online at a secure website using a preapproved proctor system or at an institutional testing site. Online testing could speed faculty response time and give faculty the opportunity to provide student feedback directly through the student's e-mail account in the LMS. Students should be able to access proctor criteria, and proctors would be able to submit application forms for approval online.
- Help links—Links should be located on each LMS page to allow students to e-mail support and helpdesk functions.
- Books and other supplies—Links to online book ordering should be included on a program website so that students can order books and have them delivered by mail.
- FAQs and other information—Information and answers to questions should be accessible on a "just in time" basis providing a rapid response to the immediate needs of learners.

(3) Faculty hiring, support, and development:

- Hiring and compensation—Determine the model(s) for faculty hiring and compensation through academic departments or the department that oversees online education. Will faculty be hired under the same criteria as classroom faculty, or must they possess online teaching experience? Will faculty be compensated for online course development as well as for teaching the course? Will they be paid the rate same as for teaching in the classroom? If courses exceed capacity, will instructors receive additional compensation, or will new sections be added?
- Scheduling and course capacity—Determine the policy on seating capacity in online courses, and the minimum and maximum enrollments. What is the course cancellation policy?
- Staffing models—Determine whether faculty members will teach online as part of their regular teaching load, or in addition to their regular teaching load for supplemental earnings. Some schools support partnerships, such as faculty and graduate student partnerships in which a faculty member (the content expert) and a graduate student (the course developer with some technical expertise) work together to develop a course. Often, the faculty

member teaches the course and the graduate student serves as a teaching assistant, or the student teaches the course under the guidance of the faculty member. Finally, instructors are frequently hired on a part-time or adjunct faculty basis from outside the institution to teach online in a specific area of expertise.

- Curriculum development—Determine where the responsibility for online education resides at the institution: in the schools, in the departments, or in a centralized unit that oversees online education? Who will approve online course development? Who will determine and approve which courses/programs are developed online? Will it be the same process as for standard face-to-face delivered courses and programs? Who will determine criteria and standards for assessing whether an online course is complete, of high quality, and ready to be offered to students?
- Assessment and standards—Determine how online education is incorporated into the institution's accreditation process. How are quality of teaching evaluated and student learning outcomes assessed? Have these processes been customized for the unique attributes of online education?
- Budgeting and revenue—Determine the source(s) of funding online education and which unit(s) receive the revenue. Will development costs be funded centrally or by individual departments or schools? What are the institutions' current and expected revenues from online enrollments?
- Faculty portal—Provide online program information, FAQs, teaching tips, calendars, schedules, best practices and faculty expectations, and other information required on an as-needed basis by faculty.

CONCLUSION

Online teaching is an opportunity to rediscover the role of a teacher in any discipline. The transition process is one of many stages of discovery and one that involves the construction of new communities: the community of learners and the faculty community. The key to success, above and beyond disciplinary expertise, is the construction of interactive elements that engage the learner. The extent to which faculty members are provided the support resources and network will effect the timeliness and quality of the teaching and learning experiences, and ultimately the satisfaction of the teacher and students. The content presented in this chapter was selected for the purpose of introducing new online instructors to the many questions and challenges they will face.

NOTE

1. Rubric created by Cindy McCourt.

BIBLIOGRAPHY

Anderson, Terry, Liam Rourke, D. Randy Garrison, and Walter Archer. 2001. "Assessing Teaching Presence in a Computer Conferencing Context." *Journal of Asynchronous Learning Networks* 5 (2): 5.

Garrison, D. Randy, Terry Anderson, and Walter Archer. 2000. "Critical Inquiry in a Text-Based Environment: Computer Conferencing in Higher Education." *The Internet and Higher Education* 2 (2–3): 1–19.

Kearsley, Greg, and Robert Blomeyer. "Preparing K–12 Teachers to Teach Online." *Greg Kearsley's Home Page*. Accessed March 26, 2012. http://home.sprynet.com/~gkearsley/TeachingOnline.htm.

Salmon, Gilly. 2004. *E-tivities: The Key to Active Online Learning*. Oxford: RoutledgeFalmer.

Schmidt, Klaus, and Dan Brown. 2004. "A Model to Integrate Online Teaching and Learning Tools into the Classroom." *The Journal of Technology Studies* 30 (2): 86–92. http://scholar.lib.vt.edu/ejournals/JOTS/v30/v30n2/pdf/schmidt.pdf.

SUGGESTED READING

Conrad, Rita-Marie, and J. Ana Donaldson. 2004. *Engaging the Online Learner: Activities and Resources for Creative Instruction*. San Francisco: John Wiley & Sons.

Kassop, Mark. 2003. "Ten Ways Online Education Matches, or Surpasses, Face-to-Face Learning." *The Technology Source* (May/June).

Ko, Susan, and Steve Rossen. 2004. *Teaching Online: A Practical Guide*. Boston: Houghton Mifflin Company.

McQuiggan, Carol A. 2007. "The Role of Faculty Development in Online Teaching's Potential to Question Teaching Beliefs and Assumptions." *Online Journal of Distance Learning Administration, Volume X, Number III*, Fall 2007, University of West Georgia, Distance Education Center. http://www.westga.edu/~distance/ojdla/fall103/mcquiggan103.htm.

Scaffolded Writing and Reviewing in the Disciplines (SWoRD), https://sites.google.com/site/swordlrdc/.

3

Learning Technologies

Christinger Tomer

INTRODUCTION

In online education, as in all other forms of education, pedagogy and the desire to learn are paramount. However, information technologies constitute an inseparable and defining element of online education, inasmuch as the design and functionality of the technologies that are used in online instruction shape every aspect of teaching and learning, and the systems in use and the choices that those systems influence almost every aspect of teaching and learning.

For the past fifteen years or so, the learning management system (LMS), which is basically a content management and file-sharing system that has been outfitted to support teaching and learning activities, has been at the technological center of online education. In recent years, the LMS has been widely and extensively supplemented by social media, most notably blogs and wikis; network-based file-sharing and presentation systems; telecommunications technologies; and systems for creating, storing, and making available audio and video recordings. Nevertheless, the LMS remains the core system of most online programs, serving mainly as a platform for the delivery of lecture notes and readings and as the medium for course-related discussion forums.

The staying power of the LMS may be attributed in large measure to its relative simplicity (and stability) as a computing platform; the ability to link the LMS across campuswide networks with other important systems, such as authentication and registration systems; and the fact that the ways in which LMSs tend to enclose and protect online learning spaces coincide with the intellectual property interests of host institutions and of the publishers through whom those institutions' libraries procure e-books, e-journals, and databases. As online education has grown and online pedagogy has become more mature and more sophisticated, complaints about the limited functionality and scope of learning management systems have begun to mount. But no clearly delineated alternative has yet emerged, suggesting that the LMS will remain the core technology of online education for the foreseeable future and that major changes in the technological basis for online education will continue to occur in other, peripheral domains.

LEARNING MANAGEMENT SYSTEMS

Definitions abound, but in general an LMS is a software application or, more frequently, a web-based technology that has been designed and is used to plan, implement, and assess specific learning processes. Typically, such systems provide instructors with ways to create and deliver content, monitor student participation, and assess student performance. In addition, learning management systems almost always provide students with interactive features, such as threaded discussions and discussion forums.[1]

The LMS has been a key factor in the development of online education, so much so that it is often difficult to divorce discussions of online learning and its assessment from those discussions concerned with the design and functions of the LMS.

In recent years, owing in significant part to services growing out of continuing increases in the bandwidth available to end-users, the LMS has often been integrated with or linked to learning content management systems (LCMS). Under an LCMS, educational content is created or uploaded to a central system, tagged, and then formatted. In most instances, the content, usually in the form of text documents but also including audio and video recordings, interactive demonstrations, and so forth, is linked to a single course shell, but one of the aims of the LCMS is to facilitate the reuse of learning objects by placing assets within a structured setting that is linked to but otherwise separate from the LMS.

As a result, recent editions of the Blackboard system, for example, feature the "Content Collection," an LCMS based on the open-source Apache Tomcat web server, with the so-called WebDAV extensions enabled. Under the LMS-only model, content is imported into or linked to a specific course shell and is reproduced only when the course is cloned. Under the model that integrates the LMS and LCMS, a folder of materials relating to a specific learning activity or academic policy may be linked not just to a single course but to as many courses as is desired, thus increasing the efficiency of course design and implementation and reducing what would otherwise be unnecessary duplication in the file storage system.[2]

In the last ten years or so, the LMS has been developed in both the proprietary and open-source software environments. In the proprietary environment, Blackboard has achieved a dominant position, in part by absorbing significant competitors such Angel and WebCT.[3] At this writing, only Desire2Learn and eCollege offer meaningful competition within the proprietary sector.[4, 5] According to the 2010 report of the Campus Computing Project, Blackboard holds about 57 percent of the market. Desire2Learn has a 10 percent share of the market, with eCollege holding about 3 percent of the market. (In recent years, the strength of Blackboard's position has slipped considerably, declining at least 10 percent in market share between 2008–2010. The reasons for this decline are not completely understood, but it seems reasonable to imagine that it has been induced by the combined effects of an economic recession, higher licensing fees, and increasingly attractive alternatives, particularly in the open-source sector.[6])

In the open-source environment, Moodle, an instructor-oriented platform based on constructivist learning models, has emerged as the leading LMS, holding about

11 percent of the overall market.[7, 8] Moodle's popularity is based in part on the fact that it will run on Linux, UNIX, OS X, and Microsoft Windows platforms, and in even greater measure on its modular design and on the wide array of modules, plugins, and themes that have been created by an allied developer community.[9] One module, for example, supports SMS-based communication with a Moodle course from a smartphone running the Android operating system; others support webcasting, the creation of concept maps, and tag cloud generation. There are modules that allow an administrator to integrate Moodle with content management systems (such as Drupal and Joomla), use repository systems such as Fedora Commons as a learning content storage system, embed Twitter in course communications, and provide server-side support for media presentation and playback. Even more important, the Moodle developer community has created hundreds of content-based modules, packages, and other resources supporting teaching and learning in many different subject areas. Finally, Moodle is supported by a community-based documentation project, Moodle Docs, that has produced a series of highly useful online manuals for both administrators and instructors.

Sakai, a Java-based system developed by a consortium of major universities, is the only other important LMS under open-source development, holding a market share slightly below 5 percent. Sakai began in 2004 with a grant from the Andrew Mellon Foundation to build what was labelled a "collaboration and learning environment."[10] The founders included the University of Michigan, MIT, Stanford, and Indiana University, as well as the Open Knowledge Initiative. Each of the founding institutions had previously developed a custom (or "homegrown") course management system, and the Sakai Project represented an effort to leverage the collective expertise and experience of the educational technologists who had built these custom systems and create a new platform for learning management.

Perhaps the most notable feature of Sakai is that while it has all of the functions and services associated with course management systems, it has also been designed to support collaborative and research-oriented activities, making it the learning management system perhaps best suited to the support of graduate education, particularly at the seminar level. In 2011, in addition to the ongoing development of what is known as the Sakai CLE, the Sakai Project has introduced a new system, the Sakai Open Academic Environment (OAE). Sakai OAE extends key motifs of the CLE system, focusing on support for content authoring, sharing, and reuse and shifting the user's focus from the site to learning and group activities.

The remainder of the LMS market is made up of proprietary systems (with miniscule market shares); homegrown systems; and efforts to adapt open-source content management systems to serve as teaching and learning environments, including a number of initiatives involving Drupal and Joomla, the most popular of the open-source content management systems, and Plone, which is the basis for the open courseware system developed by MIT and now used by a substantial number of colleges and universities. In the area of homegrown systems, it is worth noting that the University of Phoenix, which has an enrollment of 400,000 students, uses a homegrown system and is planning a new system that has been dubbed the "Learning Genome Project."[11].

SOCIAL MEDIA IN ONLINE LEARNING: BLOGS AND WIKIS

Owing to the relative inflexibility of LMSs and what is perceived to be the inadequacy of their communications capabilities, there has been considerable interest lately in exploiting Web 2.0 environments and resources to increase levels of student engagement and collaboration.[12] The problem, according to a growing number of instructors, is that "the features of LMSs may overtly or subtly align the institutional processes with the software rather than having the systems serve the requirements of the institution" (Sclater 2008, 3). The constraints that this state of affairs imposes has prompted interest in using various social networking tools and/or web-based applications to extend online courses and blend institutional resources with personal learning environments.[13] While the use of external resources is in many instances changing the nature of the online course, the trend has problematic elements, not least because there are no useful standards to guide their deployment and use or to guide the capture of the course-related data generated within the context of these applications.

Learning management systems typically include blogs and wikis. For example, Blackboard uses third-party plugins, whereas Moodle supports wikis through an optional module and Sakai does so natively. However, because access is restricted when blogs and wikis are embedded in learning management systems, and learning management systems are viewed increasingly in negative terms, instructors commonly prefer to mount blogs and wikis outside of the LMS framework and the attendant authentication schemes. Options abound, but the best ones in terms of adaptability and robustness entail the use of two open-source systems, WordPress and Mediawiki.

WordPress is a blogging platform that has been under continuous development since 2003 and has been used extensively in recent years; according to WordPress.org, as of early 2011, the software had been downloaded 32.5 million times.[14] WordPress is based on a template processor, and it features integrated link management, multifaceted categorization, tagging, trackback, pingback, a plugin architecture that extends its functionality beyond the basic installation, and a permalink structure that renders content easily assimilated by search engines.[15,16] Recently, WordPress has also incorporated an administrative infrastructure that allows updates, plugins, and themes to be installed and configured directly from the so-called "dashboard." Mediawiki, which was developed by the Wikimedia Foundation and is the software platform for all of its projects, including Wikipedia, Wiktionary and Wikinews, is highly customizable, with thousands of settings, extensions, and bots that have been developed to assist in editing the content of sites.[17,18]

Other tools that foster collaboration and communication outside the framework of the LMS are rising in popularity among online instructors and students. These include web-based productivity tools such as Google Docs; presentation media such as SlideShare and Scribd; Twitter and other micro-messaging services; VoIP (usually in the form of Skype); and web conferencing platforms such as Adobe Connect, Elluminate, WebEx, and Wimba. How these applications are used and the extent to which their use influences online education varies widely, but there can be no doubt that in their efforts to engage students, online instructors and programs are looking with increasing frequency to third-party applications that promote collaboration and interaction. Today, owing to pricing structures and features sets that are often aimed at business markets, web-based video conferencing is not yet a common feature in online education. But given the ongoing expansion of bandwidth availability, the significant improvements in overall performance that are expected to be a product of the conversion of the Internet to IPv6, and the development of applications designed primarily for educational use, it seems reasonable to think that within just a few years, video conferencing will assume a ubiquity in online education now reserved for LMSs.

PODCASTING AND LECTURE CAPTURE/PLAYBACK

As has been true of many other services, the widespread availability and increasing speeds of broadband Internet services have transformed online education, making it possible to integrate audio recordings and streaming video into courses.

It began with podcasting. What we now call "podcasts"—the term is a portmanteau combining "pod" from Apple's iPod and "broadcasting"—began to appear in the late 1990s, but the format did not achieve widespread use until 2004–2005. Identified with but not limited to media played back on Apple's iPod, podcasts typically have been audio recordings produced in a standardized file format—the most widely employed format being the MP3, developed by the Motion Picture Experts Group as part of the MPEG-1 standard—and made available through syndication technologies such as ATOM, RSS, or the proprietary iTunes.

Today, podcasting is increasingly a medium for the distribution of enhanced audio and video as well as audio-only recordings, and it is popular within the computer and publishing industries because it affords some degree of control over the distribution of content. But podcasting is also being complemented by "webcasting," which refers to media files that are distributed over the Internet through a streaming media technology to an audience of simultaneous listeners and/or viewers. In most educational settings, webcasts are based on recordings that have been created using a lecture capture system. (Live webcasts are produced less frequently, because the technical conditions that must be guaranteed in order to end users to have access of acceptable quality are much more difficult to achieve, and in many education settings asynchronous delivery, under which throughput requirements are lesser and more flexible, is preferred, in part because it conforms to the models being used for participation in online courses and programs.)

A lecture capture system is a set of technologies that are configured and used to preserve the audio and/or visual aspects of a presentation in a digital format. Typically, the capabilities of lecture capture systems include the publication of presentations, asynchronous viewing, and remote viewing. However, lecture capture systems are developing rapidly, and a number of them now also include other important features, including synchronous broadcasting, real-time messaging, and annotation services.

Lecture capture systems fall into three categories. First of all, there are systems designed primarily for personal use. A number of these systems are available free-of-charge and provide limited web-based storage and playback capabilities. Examples of such systems include Jing and Screencast-O-Matic, each of which offers free and premium services.[19, 20]

The second class of lecture capture systems are based on applications running on personal computers; unlike the systems designed primarily for personal use, however, the systems in this category, which include Adobe Captivate and Camtasia, produce recordings of higher quality, offer sophisticated editorial capabilities, and support delivery in a number of standardized video formats.[21, 22] Perhaps more to the point, even when users of these applications have only limited skill, they are able to produce recordings that meet high qualitative standards in the online learning environment.

The third category consists of lecture capture systems designed to support large-scale use across an institution or organization, which generally produce commercial-grade recordings. Probably the foremost (and best-established) system in this category is SonicFoundry's MediaSite, which supports lecture capture and webcasting.[23] One of MediaSite's distinguishing characteristics is that it relies on proprietary equipment for recording and proprietary software for delivery. Advocates of MediaSite argue that the carefully aligned development of hardware and software results in recordings of high quality. Critics contend that recordings of comparable quality can be made at significantly lower cost through the use of off-the-shelf recording equipment and delivered with equal efficiency by less expensive servers. Panopto, originally developed at Carnegie Mellon University, is effectively a response to MediaSite's putative shortcomings, in that it has been developed to use generic video equipment and computing technology in order to provide institutional consumers with a less expensive alternative.[24] (See below a captured frame from a Panopto recording that was made at the School of Information Sciences, University of Pittsburgh. No archivists were harmed in the process.)

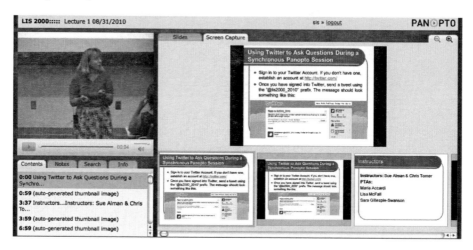

In a related vein, a group calling itself the Opencast Community, which is "working together to explore, develop, define and document best practices and technologies for management of audiovisual content in academia," has developed a software system for lecture capture called "Matterhorn."[25] Matterhorn is an open-source system, available free-of-charge, that has been designed to capture lectures, manage recordings, serve designated distribution channels such as YouTube and iTunes University, and provide a user interface.

RELEVANT TECHNICAL STANDARDS

Standardization is an essential aspect of technological development, because it increases efficiencies, enhances interoperability, and fosters competition. Efforts to form useful technical standards for online education have yielded the Shareable Content Object Reference Model (SCORM) and the Common Cartridge format, but with mixed results. SCORM is a set of specifications developed under the Advanced Distributed Learning Initiative (ADL). The goal of SCORM is to create learning objects that are reuseable; interoperable (meaning that the content will function under different hardware and software configurations); durable (meaning that the content does not require modification after software systems upgrades or changes); accessible; maintainable (meaning that the content can be altered without redesign, reconfiguration or recoding); and adaptable. SCORM 2004 incorporates rules that specify the order in which a learner may or should experience learning objects. Known under SCORM as "sequencing," these rules constrain learners to a fixed set of paths through the training material, permit them to "bookmark" their progress when taking breaks, and control students' progression through testing and performance standards.[26]

Common Cartridge, developed by the IMS Global Learning Consortium (GLC), was conceived to be an extension of SCORM, intended to advance the standardization of learning content packaging. According to the IMS GLC, Common Cartridge consists of "standards for organization, publishing, distribution, delivery, search and authorization of a wide variety of collections of digital learning content, applications, and associated online discussion forums used as the basis for or in support of online learning of any type."[27] Based on the Dublin Core Metadata Element Set, Common Cartridge also represents an effort to expand the definition of learning objects, incorporating tests, distributed content, interactions with external tools, applications and services, access rights, and collaborative forums.[28]

The difference between SCORM and Common Cartridge is that SCORM is based on computer-based training (CBT) models that assume little or no interaction, whereas Common Cartridge "was designed to allow the use of learning material in the interactive, collaborative environment of students and teachers, nowadays not necessarily gathered in the same spatial location but communicating and interacting in an equivalent way."[29]

Conflicts arose recently when the IMS GLC concluded that SCORM was too narrow in its scope, inasmuch as SCORM development is focused on the needs of contractors associated with the US Department of Defense and its Advanced Distributed Learning Initiative (ADL), and consequently abandoned support for SCORM in the ongoing development of Common Cartridge. In response, it has been proposed that a new version of SCORM, tentatively known as SCORM 2.0, will extend its definition of interoperability beyond the conventional learning platform and entail no assumptions about the nature of content or systems.[30]

As commentators have noted, the obvious problem with this state of affairs is that having two competing standards means having no standard at all. The degrees of freedom enjoyed by educational technologists, particularly when they propose to move learning objects from one platform to another, are currently limited. (It should be noted, however, that one of the factors tempering problems of standardization and interoperability is the limited interest among many educators in reuseable learning objects. It is not clear why such interest is not greater, but it seems reasonable to imagine that it stems in large part from the failure of many instructors to make the transition from traditional models of basic course organization—e.g., lectures, readings, papers, and examinations—to object-oriented views of the same content, as well from a lack of adequate technical support, particularly in terms of infrastructure and software.)

STARTING AN ONLINE EDUCATION PROGRAM

When starting an online program, the first and most important choice from the perspective of both administrators and instructors is the selection of a learning management system. While proprietary systems offer many advantages (and may be preferred by organizations pursuing a well-funded commitment to building a large-scale online program), the open-source options are decidedly better for most schools because they entail reduced financial risk and more options in terms of installation and configuration. Of the open-source options available, Moodle should be preferred owing to the simplicity of its core installation and administration, although, as noted above, Sakai is an excellent choice for programs focusing on delivery under smaller enrollments combined with interactive teaching strategies.

Decisions about the deployment of a lecture capture system are more complex. If software like Camtasia, Adobe Captivate, or Jing is used, there are significant per-seat licensing costs for producers, there are substantial requirements in terms of technical support, and there is also the cost of providing servers capable of storing and streaming the content generated by instructors. If a larger scale system is deployed, issues of cost, production and technical support, and the capacities of network infrastructures come into play. Perhaps more to the point, the widespread use of lecture capture systems and the increasing use of video conferencing technologies raise expectations among instructors and students alike, and it is possible that online education has reached a point in its development beyond which it is no longer reasonable to imagine offering a program of relatively higher quality without the support and added expense of such systems.

Schools considering the launch of an online learning program should consider cloud computing as the basis for the initiative. Why? Because cloud computing, which is defined by the National Institute of Standards and Technology as "a model for enabling convenient, on-demand network access to a shared pool of configurable computing resources (e.g., networks, servers, storage, applications, and services) that can be rapidly provisioned and released with minimal management effort or service provider interaction," provides a reliable and economically rational approach to computer provisioning and enables its users to undertake computationally significant initiatives with little or no up-front costs and to incur ongoing expenses on the basis of actual, as opposed to anticipated, demands for computing resources.[31]

For example, through Amazon Web Services (AWS), it is possible to launch a server, outfit it with a public Internet address, and begin the process of installing and configuring services within 15–20 minutes.[32] An administrator familiar with the AWS administrative console could reasonably expect to have the core installation for a system such as Moodle installed and running in another 10–15 minutes. Because such an operation can be undertaken without any investment in server hardware or network infrastructure (and requires only Internet access and an account on Amazon), the cost of an exploratory initiative is nominal. What is more important, an online learning management system based on open-source software could be provisioned for a basic monthly cost of well under $100, with additional costs accruing as a function of the extent of demand on the server for computing cycles and size of the files stored on the system, and without the depreciation of much of the hardware that would otherwise be needed.[33]

In Kentucky, the Pike County School District is using cloud-based services in lieu of both servers and desktops for students. The district estimates that provisioning computing and networking on this basis will reduce costs by half over a five-year cycle. Of equal importance, it is believed that as a result of the transition to cloud computing aspects of teaching and learning operate at a substantially higher level, because the availability and functionality of virtual machines can be guaranteed to a degree that the Pike County School District could not when its primary approach to provisioning was based on locally maintained computers.[34]

In the end, the most important factor in deploying technologies in support of online education is providing instructors and students with systems that are easy to use and which can be adapted to the changing requirements of each constituency. Perhaps the most important lesson that we have learned thus far, at least technologically, is that the limitations of learning management systems are real and significant, and that they bound online education in ways that are ultimately undesirable. The challenge ahead is to create and deploy new learning technologies that can be adapted quickly and substantially to the needs of teachers and learners.

NOTES

1. See http://searchcio.techtarget.com/definition/learning-management-system.

2. One of the advantages of the LCMS model used by Blackboard is that because it is based on widely used, well-documented open-source software, it can be effectively replicated in other settings. So, although an LMS such as Moodle does not provide a LCMS as an integral feature, it is relatively simple to provide such a service in parallel to the LMS through the installation and configuration of Apache Tomcat.

3. See http://www.blackboard.com/.

4. See http://www.desire2learn.com/.

5. See http://www.ecollege.com/index.learn.

6. From "The 2010 Managing Online Education Survey," *The Campus Computing Project*, p. 12. See http://www.campuscomputing.net/.

7. Moodle is the abbreviation for Modular Object-Oriented Dynamic Learning Environment.

8. According to Moodle, in 2011, there were 54,112 registered sites across the world, offering slightly more than 4.5 million courses involving 1.1 million instructors and 43.1 million students.

9. Moodle is also available as downloadable appliance from Bitnami. (See http://bitnami. org/.) This version comes with the supporting Web server and database management system fully configured at installation, easing the set up requirements for organizations that want to experiment with Moodle, or which lack the technical expertise necessary to install the system from source code or binaries.

10. See http://sakaiproject.org/.

11. Kolowich, Steve. The Thinking LMS. *Inside Higher Education*, October 18, 2010. (Last accessed on June 16, 2011.)

12. Sclater, Niall. Web 2.0, Personal Learning Environments, and the Future of Learning Management Systems. *EDUCAUSE Center for Applied Research (ECAR) Research Bulletin* 2008 (2008): 2.

13. Dron, Jon. "Any Color You Like, As Long As It's Blackboard" (paper presented at the World Conference on E-Learning in Corporate, Government, Healthcare, and Higher Education (ELEARN), Honolulu, Hawaii, October 2006).

14. See http://wordpress.org/.

15. A trackback is one of three types of linkback methods for Web authors to request notification when somebody links to one of their documents. Authors are thus able to keep track of who is linking (or referring) to their articles. Pingbacks refer to an XML-RPC-based "push" mechanism, whereby all the links in a published article can be updated when the article is published.

16. A permalink is a URL that remains unchanged indefinitely. The term is most often associated with blogging and content syndication software.

17. See http://www.mediawiki.org/wiki/MediaWiki/.

18. A wiki is a website that allows the creation and editing of any number of interlinked web pages via a web browser using a simplified markup language or a WYSIWYG text editor. Wikis are typically powered by wiki software and used collaboratively by multiple users. Examples include community websites, corporate intranets, knowledge management systems, and note services.

19. See http://www.techsmith.com/jing/.

20. The URL for Jing is http://www.techsmith.com/Jing/; the URL for Screen-O-Matic is http://www.screencast-o-matic.com/.

21. See http://www.adobe.com/products/captivate.html.

22. See http://www.techsmith.com/camtasia/.

23. See http://www.sonicfoundry.com/mediasite/.

24. See http://www.panopto.com/.

25. The Opencast Community is an international collaborative whose members include Columbia University, Penn State, Stanford, the Australian National University, Cambridge University, the University of Sao Paulo, and Ben-Gurion University.

26. See Gonzalez-Barbone, Victor, and Luis Anido-Rifon. From SCORM to Common Cartridge: A step forward. *Computers & Education* 54 (2010) 88–102.

27. Gonzalez/Anido, p. 98.

28. Britain, Sandy. "On the Relationship between Pedagogical Design and Content Management in eLearning." From *Content Management for E-Learning*. Edited by Nuria Ferrer and Julia Minguillion. New York: Springer, 2011, pp. 55–69.

29. Gonzalez-Barbone, op cit., p. 98.

30. Julià Minguillón, et al. "From Content Management to E-Learning Content Repositories." From Content Management for E-Learning. Edited by Edited by Nuria Ferrer and Julia Minguillion. New York: Springer, 2011, pp. 2–41.

31. Mell, Peter and Tom Grance. *The NIST Definition of Cloud Computing*. Version 15, 10-7-09; see also Owens, Dustin. Securing Elasticity in the Cloud. *Communications of the ACM* 53 (June 2010): 50.

32. See http://aws.amazon.com/.

33. Sultan, Nabil. Cloud computing for education: A new dawn? *International Journal of Information Management* 30 (2010) 109–16.

34. Sultan, op cit., p. 112.

REFERENCES

Alfonso, Julià Minguillón, Miguel Angel Sicilia, and Brian Lamb. 2011. "From Content Management to E-Learning Content Repositories." In *Content Management for E-Learning*, edited by Núria Ferran Ferrer and Julià Minguillón Alfonso, 2–41. New York: Springer.

Britain, Sandy. 2011. "On the Relationship between Pedagogical Design and Content Management in eLearning." In *Content Management for E-Learning*, edited by Núria Ferran Ferrer and Julià Minguillón Alfonso, 55–69. New York: Springer.

Campus Computing Project. 2010. "2010 Managing Online Education Survey." Campus Computing Project. Accessed April 2, 2012. http://www.campuscomputing.net/sites/www.campuscomputing.net/files/ManagingOnlineEd2010-ExecSummaryGraphics_1.pdf.

Dron, Jon. 2006. "Any Color You Like, As Long As It's Blackboard." Paper presented at the World Conference on E-Learning in Corporate, Government, Healthcare, and Higher Education (ELEARN), Honolulu, Hawaii, October 2006.

Gonzalez-Barbone, Victor, and Luis Anido-Rifon. 2010. "From SCORM to Common Cartridge: A Step Forward." *Computers & Education* 54: 88–102.

Kolowich, Steve. 2010. "The Thinking LMS." *Inside Higher Education*, October 18. Accessed June 16, 2011. http://www.insidehighered.com/news/2010/10/18/phoenix.

Mell, P., and Grance, T. (2011). The NIST Definition of Cloud Computing (Draft) Recommendations of the National Institute of Standards and Technology. *Nist Special Publication* 145 (6), 7. National Institute of Standards and Technology, Information Technology Laboratory. Retrieved from http://csrc.nist.gov/publications/drafts/800-145/Draft-SP-800-145_cloud-definition.pdf.

Owens, Dustin. 2010. "Securing Elasticity in the Cloud." *Communications of the ACM* 53: 50.

Sclater, Niall. 2008. "Web 2.0, Personal Learning Environments, and the Future of Learning Management Systems" (Research Bulletin, Issue 13). Boulder, CO: EDUCAUSE Center for Applied Research.

Sultan, Nabil. 2010. "Cloud Computing for Education: A New Dawn?" *International Journal of Information Management* 30: 109–16.

4

Student Assessment in Online Learning

Lorna R. Kearns

INTRODUCTION

Marta works as a high school librarian in a large public school district. She has been tasked with creating a series of self-paced online learning modules to teach students about online literacy. Using a learning management system, she will create instructional content, learning activities, and assessments for each module. Students must achieve a score of 80 percent or higher on the final quiz to receive a certificate of completion. Marta will need to align the assessments with the modules' learning objectives to provide valid evidence of mastery.

Vincent is a librarian for a community library in rural New Mexico. Recently, his library has begun getting requests to act as a test site and provide exam proctors for adult learners enrolled in a variety of online learning programs. Instructors of online courses often direct students to contact their local libraries to arrange proctoring services. For courses that focus on quantitative skills or contain a considerable amount of dense, objective content, proctored exams at remote sites can provide a good substitute for on-site, instructor-administered tests.

Janine is an academic librarian at a university that is expanding its online courses and programs. She is receiving increasing requests from online students for support in searching electronic databases to complete research papers. Unlike the many face-to-face (f2f) conversations she conducted with undergraduates about their assignment objectives just a few years ago, the growing majority of these new reference transactions take place via e-mail, chat, and even Skype. At first, Janine found it challenging to communicate effectively with these media, but she now feels she is getting better at interpreting her current patrons' needs.

The surge in online learning has created situations like these for many librarians who find themselves being asked to create online instruction and support students at a distance. To be effective at these tasks, it is important for librarians to understand the fundamentals of instructional design and assessment for online learning. This chapter focuses on assessment of student learning in online learning environments. It begins with a review of the literature of student assessment in general, proceeds to identify and explicate areas that warrant particular attention for online learning, and finishes with a set of key recommendations for practice.

THEMES IN THE LITERATURE

Simonson and colleagues (2006) summarize the different purposes that assessment serves. In addition to providing the instructor with data for assigning a grade, assessments inform both instructor and student about how closely the student has approximated a target objective. Instructors can use this information to address gaps in the instruction; students can use it to modify their learning strategies. Frequent assessments serve to reinforce key concepts and provide opportunities for practice with the material.

Bloxham and Boyd (2007) observe that assessment has a strong influence on learning and the learning process. It affects the type of effort students exert and the quality and quantity of what they learn. Snyder (1971) used the term "the hidden curriculum" to describe how students' perceptions and expectations of assessments shape their approaches to studying.

Well-designed assessments provide strong motivation to students (e.g., Black and Wiliam 1998; Seale, Chapman, and Davey, 2000). They focus students' attention on what is important and serve as prompts for students to mobilize resources and study strategies. Feedback contributes significantly in raising student achievement (Black and Wiliam 1998; Gibbs and Simpson 2004–5). To be effective, feedback should be timely, targeted, and constructive.

ASSESSMENT DESIGN PROCESS

Instructional alignment is a fundamental tenet of good instructional design. It is the notion that instruction should align with assessment: what is taught should be tested, and what is tested needs to be taught (Cohen 1987). The three essential elements of instructional alignment are learning objectives, instructional activities, and assessments. Learning objectives specify what the student should be expected to accomplish at the completion of the instruction. Assessments provide evidence of this accomplishment, and activities provide practice opportunities for students in developing the competence needed to achieve a specified level of mastery. Figure 4.1 illustrates this relationship.

Developing learning objectives is a precursor to creating assessments. Wiggins and McTighe (1998) argue for a backward design process that includes these steps:

1. Identify desired results. (Learning objectives)
2. Determine acceptable evidence. (Assessments)
3. Plan learning experiences and instruction. (Learning activities)

The planning process is backward because the assessments are specified *before* the activities are designed. Students advancing through the process, however, complete learning activities *before* taking assessments.

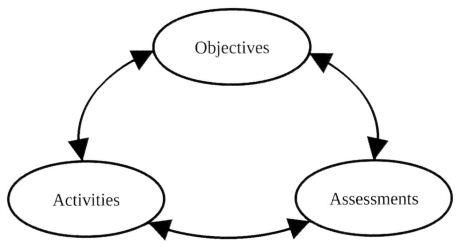

Figure 4.1.
Instructional alignment of learning objectives, instructional activities, and assessments.

ISSUES IN ASSESSMENT OF ONLINE LEARNING

The principles mentioned in the preceding section are generalizable to both the online and f2f learning environments. Thus, they should inform instructional design decisions in both environments. Even so, the research from which they are derived was conducted, for the most part, in traditional learning environments. This section focuses specifically on the context of online learning, highlighting both the challenges and affordances it presents.

Hannafin and colleagues (2003) reinforce the proposition that assessments act as signals to students about what is important in a course. In web-based learning environments, where students are physically distant from their instructors and other classmates, this phenomenon is even more pronounced. In such environments, course design carries perhaps more weight than in f2f courses where students have numerous opportunities to informally interact with their instructor and one another.

Liang and Creasy (2004) point out that informal assessment may be difficult for online instructors because they do not have regular opportunities for face-to-face interaction with their students. Thus, their ability to monitor students' understanding is limited. On the other hand, since all communication in an online course is mediated by technology, the special affordances offered by such technology are worth investigating. Online discussion, for example, a commonly assessed activity in online courses, is often used as a substitute for classroom discussion. It is perhaps a better assessment tool than f2f discussion because the postings students make to the discussion board create an evolving document of participation that an instructor can review. And, because online discussion is asynchronous (i.e., a time lag exists between participant responses), it gives students the occasion to reflect on and refine their ideas before posting. Finally, the record it provides can be used by students as reference material when completing assignments.

A number of additional issues surface repeatedly in the literature of assessment in online learning. These include the importance of activities and assessments that enable self-monitoring and promote self-regulation (Booth et al. 2003; Kim, Smith, and

Maeng 2008; Robles and Braathen 2002); peer and group assessment practices (Booth et al. 2003; Kim, Smith, and Maeng 2008); the need to incorporate authentic assessment into online courses (e.g., Assessment and Online Teaching 2002; Kim, Smith, and Maeng 2008; Robles and Braathen 2002); and concern about cheating and plagiarism in online learning (Simonson et al. 2006).

DIMENSIONS OF ASSESSMENT IN ONLINE LEARNING

It is useful to refer to dimensions of assessment in describing a particular set of assessment choices. McAlpine (2002) identifies five dimensions:

1. Formative/summative
2. Formal/informal
3. Final/continuous
4. Process/product
5. Convergent/divergent

Just as we might describe a person's appearance using dimensions like height and weight, we can also describe assessments using a subset of these dimensions. For example, a final exam composed of multiple-choice questions is a summative, formal, convergent assessment, while an exercise in which students submit drafts of a research project for peer review is a formative, informal, convergent assessment.

The formative/summative dimension indicates whether the primary purpose of the assessment is to inform students about their ongoing progress towards a goal or to provide data to the instructor at a specified end point about a student's mastery of a skill or concept. As Robert Stake has said, "When the cook tastes the soup, that's formative; when the guests taste the soup, that's summative" (quoted in Scriven 1991, 169). Because online students work on their own without the regular f2f company of their peers or instructor, it is important to provide opportunities for them to assess their own learning. Such opportunities not only help students to monitor their progress in a particular course but also contribute to the development of an orientation to effective lifelong learning.

Formal assessments are graded activities. Students know when they are being formally assessed. Criteria for success are usually quite explicit for formal assessments. Conversely, in an informal assessment, students may not even know that they are being observed. Instructors use informal assessments to gather information about a student's progress toward a learning goal. In the classroom, instructors can collect informal assessment data by listening to students' comments and questions. When students are physically distant from their instructor, as in most online classes, opportunities for informal assessments are limited. Thus, in an online class, care must be taken to design activities that provide these data. What we measure along this dimension is the degree to which the student is aware of and able to prepare for being graded. Because this dimension is continuous and not bipolar, we can have assessments that are more or less informal depending on the weight assigned to the activity. Assessments that contribute a large percentage to the overall course grade are much more formal than those that contribute a few percentage points.

A final assessment is exactly what it sounds like: an assessment that is conducted at the very end of a course. It is high-stakes and comprehensive. Assessments of this sort are often found in professional programs that require credentialing, such as law or medicine. Continuous, or ongoing, assessments, on the other hand, are administered more frequently throughout a course, each one contributing a smaller percentage to the overall course grade. The multiple data points they yield provide benchmarks of students' baseline work and documentation of developing mastery.

Using the process/product dimension, an assessment can measure the quality of an artifact, something produced by the student, or it can measure aspects of the process the student used to produce it. To improvise on Stake's remark about the formative and summative assessment of soup, one could say that tasting the soup is a product-oriented assessment, whereas watching the cook make the soup is a process-oriented assessment. If we measure this dimension along a continuum, we can position graded online discussion closer to the process than product end of the continuum because it assesses students not only on the quality of their postings but also on how they interact with their peers and affect the discussion process.

The final dimension in McAlpine's framework is convergent/divergent. Convergent assessments are those for which there is a small set of correct answers. Convergent assessments include quizzes and exams composed of multiple-choice, true/false, matching, and short-answer questions. Convergent assessments lend themselves to being automatically graded. Divergent assessments, on the other end of the spectrum, are those for which there are multiple correct responses. They usually require interpretation and often give students the opportunity to apply their understanding in individualistic ways. Assessments that are divergent include term papers, response papers, portfolios, and group projects. Some authors refer to this dimension as traditional/alternative (e.g., Dikli 2003). Traditional assessments comprise objective tests and quizzes, whereas alternative assessments comprise the divergent assessment methods mentioned above and are rooted in a constructivist philosophy that values active, collaborative learning. A subcategory of alternative assessment is authentic assessment. Assessments of this type require students to apply concepts learned in class to novel situations likely to be encountered in the real world.

ASSESSMENT METHODS FOR ONLINE LEARNING

This section reviews methods of assessment, both traditional and authentic, that can be used in online learning environments.

Traditional Assessment Methods

Although it is sometimes suggested that traditional assessments be reserved for measuring lower-level learning (e.g., Robles and Braathen 2002), it is possible, with care, to construct objective test questions that evaluate higher-level learning such as application and analysis (Burton et al. 1991). Learning levels can be classified according to Bloom's Taxonomy (Bloom 1987) as shown in Figure 4.2.

Consider the two multiple-choice questions shown in Table 4.1. Question 1 is a recall-level question. It asks the learner to differentiate among the four possible answers and exclusively identify the one that means the same as the symbol given in the question stem. As an example of a higher-level test item, question 2 presents the student with a novel problem: how to find links to online quizzes about information literacy. This question requires students to analyze the problem, generate some possible

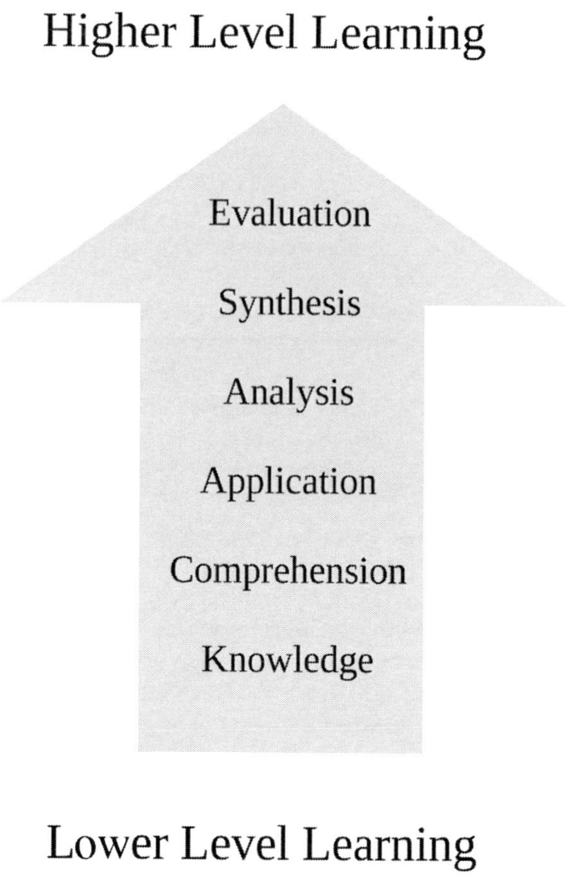

Higher Level Learning

Evaluation

Synthesis

Analysis

Application

Comprehension

Knowledge

Lower Level Learning

Figure 4.2.
Levels of learning according to Bloom's Taxonomy.
(Bloom 1987)

correct solutions, and then evaluate which of the four choices most closely matches their set of correct solutions. Both types of questions can be effective in online learning environments. Recall and comprehension questions can be used in pretests to assess students' current knowledge and in posttests to identify gaps in understanding. Higher-level questions, those that assess application, analysis, and evaluation, provide students with practice in applying concepts to novel cases.

If you use traditional assessments, your learning management system should offer several options for its implementation. For example, you may set a time limit on when the test is available to students (e.g., three days) and on how long students have to complete the test once they start (e.g., two hours). You may allow multiple attempts for ungraded quizzes or require that students complete the entire test in one sitting with no opportunity to retake. You may also provide automated feedback during or immediately after a quiz. Feedback may take the form of simply displaying the correct answer after a student completes an item, or you may create feedback for each distractor (wrong answer) as well, explaining why a particular distractor is incorrect.

Table 4.1.

Multiple choice questions for assessing lower- and higher-level knowledge

	Question	Correct Answer
1.	In a Google search, the symbol l is the same as: a. AND b. OR c. NOT d. +	b. OR
2.	Which of the following search expressions is most likely to find useful links to online quizzes about information literacy? a. information OR literacy quiz b. (information literacy) OR quiz c. "information literacy" AND quiz d. "information AND literacy" AND quiz	c. "information literacy" AND quiz

Most learning management systems enable the creation of a test item pool from which items can be randomly selected. Of course, you must first create the test pool, but you may build it over a couple of semesters until you have a target number of items, after which you can review and refine individual test items. For example, an online quiz might use a test pool of 25 items from which 15 are drawn at random and presented in random order for each student taking the test.

Even if you do not use a test pool from semester to semester and instead deploy all items in a given test, you may still randomize their order of presentation for each student. In addition, you may also choose to randomize the order of answer options for each item. While there are many cases in which *item* randomization is beneficial, there are probably fewer situations that call for the random presentation of *answer options*. When answer options have a logical or numerical order, they should be presented in that order (Haladyna 1994). Remember, when constructing multiple-choice questions, the goal is to assess the student's mastery of a specific content area, not to confuse. A strong multiple-choice question is one with a clearly stated stem and a set of answer options that neither provide clues to the correct answer nor obscure it with misleading information. Answer options will always include one correct answer and several distractors. In developing distractors, choose those that are plausible but incorrect. One strategy is to pattern distractors after the kinds of errors students commonly make. Table 4.2 provides examples of both a well-constructed and a poorly constructed multiple-choice question. Question 1 is a good multiple-choice question because it targets a high level of learning by posing a novel situation that the responder must evaluate in order to choose the correct answer. In addition, the distractor options are all plausible answers to the question. In this question, the important information is that the professor's institution does not subscribe to the journal. Therefore, the professor must seek permission from the journal to distribute the article to the class. Among the distractors are common misconceptions ranging from the mistaken belief that the professor can distribute the article because he authored it to the overly cautious perception that the institution must purchase a subscription to the journal.

Table 4.2.

Example of a well-constructed and a poorly constructed multiple choice question

	Question	Correct Answer
1.	Professor Dahlgren teaches at Southwestern State University. He wrote a journal article with a colleague from another institution. He wishes to assign the article as a reading for his class, but Southwestern State does not subscribe to the journal. What should he do to be in copyright compliance? a. Since he already has a copy of the article, he may make it available on his course site. b. He should seek permission to use the article from his co-author. c. He should seek permission to use the article from the journal in which it was published. d. He must purchase a subscription to the journal if he wishes to use the article.	c. He should seek permission to use the article from the journal in which it was published.
2.	The TEACH Act is a law that: a. requires all teachers to spend 90% of their day teaching. b. replaces the Civil Rights Act. c. redefines the terms and conditions on which accredited, nonprofit educational institutions throughout the United States may use c. copyright-protected materials in distance education. d. none of the above	c. redefines the terms and conditions on which accredited, nonprofit educational institutions throughout the United States may use copyright-protected materials in distance education.

Question 2, on the other hand, is a poorly constructed question. All four of its answer options are in conflict with Haladyna's (1994) good design principles. Option A presents a far-fetched, humorous alternative, providing a strong hint that it is incorrect. Option B is obviously wrong because the answer is not even in same subject domain as the question stem. The text of option C contains two clues that it is the correct answer: it is not only much longer than the other options, but it has been reproduced verbatim from the source text, the American Library Association (ALA) website. Finally, option D uses "none of the above" as a choice. Although frequently used as a distractor, this option does not provide an opportunity for the responder to choose the correct answer.

Authentic Assessment Methods

Authentic assessments are those which require students to complete assignments that approximate tasks they might encounter in their field of practice. These include established favorites like research papers, group or individual projects, case study analyses, and problem-solving activities. Other types of authentic assessment, such as portfolios, have emerged in the last two decades in response to calls for practices that reflect a more complete picture of student learning. Still other methods have been enabled by technology developments, including online discussion and other online collaborative work.

Research papers and other written assignments that require students to consult books, journal articles, and web sources provide an opportunity for higher-order learning at the synthesis and evaluation levels. Academic databases such as EBSCO, JSTOR, and ProQuest enable online students to retrieve journal articles through their institution's subscription to the database, and digitized e-books can be accessed via institutional subscriptions to NetLibrary. Provided that students have been appropriately educated on information legitimacy issues, the web itself can be a portal to many freely available resources for use as source material for research projects.

Group work is another commonly used authentic assessment strategy. While it offers opportunities for collaborative learning and community building, it has its disadvantages as well, the most common being the phenomenon of free riding. One way to counteract this problem is to provide team work instruction to your students in the early stages of their group work. Piezon and Donaldson (2005) recommend training that helps students to clarify roles and responsibilities and ensure that each team member has a meaningful, contributive role to play in achieving the end goal. Wikis are web-based tools that can be very effective in supporting group project work (Lamb 2004). A wiki is really nothing more than a website composed of pages created and edited by members of a team. Wikipedia is perhaps the best-known publicly available wiki, but there are dozens of other freely available web-based applications that support this kind of work. Many learning management systems have wikis of their own. Using a wiki can offset the problem of free riding because the wiki keeps track of the work submitted by individual group members.

Portfolio assessment is an assessment method in which students build a collection of documents and other instructional artifacts that they've created to demonstrate evidence of their learning within a specific domain. Although the original idea behind portfolio assessment called for a hard-copy collection of artifacts contained in a binder or presentation case, there are many examples today of electronic portfolios, or e-portfolios, built on a web-based platform such as a wiki or blog. Because it is the student's responsibility to select the items for inclusion in the portfolio, this approach is a perfect opportunity for students to critically reflect on their own work and develop a more sophisticated level of skill in self-assessment.

A final method of authentic assessment worth mentioning here is online discussion. Assessing online discussion has become a common practice in online learning environments. As the platform for dialogue, information exchange, and collaborative learning, the discussion forum is often considered the heart of an online class. Research has shown that online discussion plays an important role in student satisfaction with online courses and that grading the discussion is an important motivator for students to participate (Swan 2001). In designing discussion activities, question prompts are commonly used to initiate the discussion. When developing discussion questions, it is best to create divergent, rather than convergent, questions. Divergent questions are those for which there may be multiple responses, whereas convergent questions have a limited set of correct responses. Table 4.3 provides an example of both a convergent and divergent question. Notice that, although the convergent question is a high-level question, asking students to apply a concept to a particular

Table 4.3.

Example of a convergent and a divergent discussion question

Convergent Question	Divergent Question
There are four factors commonly used to determine "fair use." Choose one of the four factors and show how it would inform decision making about reading material for an online course.	There are four factors commonly used to determine "fair use." Using a college course with which you are familiar, either online or face-to-face, describe how the Fair Use Doctrine was used to inform decision making about reading material for the course. How did the course format (online vs. face-to-face) affect the decision?

situation, the answers will eventually begin to converge. The divergent question, on the other hand, asks students to apply a concept they learned to an example of their own choosing. Answers to this question will be less repetitive and likely lead to a more multifaceted exchange of ideas.

Along with decisions about the type of assessment methods to use, instructors must also decide how much of a contribution each assessment makes to a student's overall course grade. Table 4.4 summarizes findings from two studies showing average weights assigned to discussion, exams, and written papers. It is obvious from both studies that online discussion is being used as a graded activity in a significant number of courses.

ACADEMIC INTEGRITY IN ASSESSMENT OF ONLINE LEARNING

Stakeholders in online learning have voiced concerns about academic integrity in these environments. While the issue is certainly recognized in the literature, little empirical research has been conducted on the topic. With virtually no large-scale studies of cheating in online learning (Baron and Crooks 2005), the question remains: is cheating easier online?

Table 4.4.

Average contribution of discussion, exams, and written papers to overall course grade

Author	N	Findings
Arend (2007)	60 courses	98% used discussion, with an average weight of 17%. 83% used exams, with an average weight of 48%. 63% used papers, with an average weight of 24%.
Swan (2001)	73 courses	82% used discussion, most with a weight between 10 & 25%. 57% used exams, most with a weight between 26 & 50%. 37% used papers, most with a weight between 10 & 25%.

A recent study of f2f instruction (Vandehey, Diekhoff, and LaBeff 2007) found rates of cheating in college to have changed very little in the 20 years between 1984 and 2004. However, a study on *beliefs* about cheating (Kennedy et al. 2000) concluded that both college students and faculty *believed* that cheating was easier in distance education classes. The few studies that exist show mixed evidence. Grijalva, Kerkvliet, and Nowell (2006) found that college student self-reports of cheating for online learning were no higher than f2f student self-reports. On the other hand, Harmon and Lambrinos (2008) found that cheating was more likely to occur during unproctored exams of online courses than during proctored exams. Regardless of the frequency of cheating and plagiarism in online learning, the perception of the potential for it warrants proactive attention and oversight on the part of course designers, instructors, and administrators of online learning programs.

You can take steps to minimize academic misconduct in online courses. For high-stakes tests, you may require students to find a test proctor. Many libraries and educational institutions offer this service. Specific procedures may vary from program to program, but the overall process entails these steps:

1. The student finds a proctor site and provides contact information to the online instructor.
2. At a prearranged date and time, the student arrives at the proctor site to take the test. He/she must usually provide proof of identification.
3. If the test is not to be taken online, the instructor will send a paper copy of the test to the proctor. Whether it is online or paper based, the student takes the test in the presence of the proctor in the time allotted by the instructor. If it is paper based, the proctor sends the completed test back to the instructor.

Although this process has become quite common, it is typically reserved for high-stakes tests administered once or twice during a semester, as it can become burdensome for everyone involved if used too frequently within one course.

Recently, a web-based alternative to on-site proctoring has emerged. One company, ProctorU (http://www.proctoru.com/), offers a service whereby a student with a webcam and microphone accesses the ProctorU website, provides proof of identification to a live proctor, and takes the test while being filmed with the webcam. Dozens of colleges and universities are now using the service for their online classes.

Threats to academic integrity exist with authentic assessments as well as traditional ones. When faced with an impending deadline for a written assignment, for instance, a student may try to obtain a paper from an online term paper site. Several strategies are available to use in these situations to reduce the probability of academic misconduct and ensure that students turn in their own work:

- Use cumulative assignments that students submit over the course of the semester. This requires students to show their developing progress on a project.
- Use student participation in online discussion to benchmark their writing style and ability, or administer an early low-stakes writing assessment to use as a benchmark.
- Make use of plagiarism detection tools like Turnitin (http://turnitin.com/) or SafeAssign (http://safeassign.com/). This strategy requires students to turn in their papers to a web-based database that compares students' work to other papers in the database to see whether there are any matches.
- Develop assignments that integrate personal experiences with the topic of the paper.
- Ask students to make connections to timely, current events.

KEY RECOMMENDATIONS

Synthesizing the information presented in this chapter on purposes, methods, and dimensions of assessment, this section proposes a set of general principles to guide assessment development in multiple online learning contexts.

Align assessments with learning objectives. The right place to begin in developing assessments is with learning objectives. Start by determining what your students should accomplish as a result of the instruction. How will you measure that accomplishment? What evidence will you use? Your answers to these questions should have direct influence on the assessments you create for your course.

Use a variety of assessment methods. This is a good practice for multiple reasons. For one thing, it addresses differences in individual learning styles among students (Gaytan and McEwen 2007). It also provides a more comprehensive picture of individual student performance than any one assessment can provide (Rovai 2000) and gives students an opportunity to demonstrate multiple facets of their performance (Seale, Chapman, and Davey 2000).

Administer frequent assessments. Frequent assessments give students the opportunity to reflect on their developing mastery, providing benchmarks they can use to compare earlier and later performance. They help to reinforce correct understanding as well as identify misconceptions students may have (Simonson et al. 2006). In online learning environments, where rates of student non-completion have been higher than in f2f instruction (Levy 2007), frequent assessments may help keep students on task and in the loop.

Provide clear, complete instructions. Important for any assessment, clarity and completeness are even more essential for online learning. Online classes offer fewer chances to correct student misperceptions than in a f2f class. Because traditional assessments are usually timed tests, instructions must be crystal clear before students begin the assessment. There should be no chance that time will be wasted trying to figure out an instruction. For alternative assessments, target performance criteria should be specified and exemplars of accomplished student work provided. Setting up a discussion board specifically for student questions about assignments, activities, and assessments is a practice that gets misunderstandings out in the open and helps the instructor avoid answering the same questions multiple times via email.

Offer constructive and timely feedback. Effective feedback helps students understand what constitutes good performance, demonstrates how current performance relates to target performance, and provides information about how to close the gap between the two (Sadler 1989). Feedback must also be timely in order to be of value to student learning. Because the provision of timely feedback can be a challenging workload issue for instructors, it is worthwhile to look for opportunities for feedback that do not require the instructor to be available 24/7. Online assessments that provide automated feedback constitute one such method. Offering opportunities for peer feedback is another way to offload some of the burden from the instructor.

CONCLUSION

Important purposes served by assessment include providing the instructor with data for grading, comparing the student's performance to that of a target, identifying gaps, reinforcing key concepts, offering practice opportunities, and focusing students' attention.

Lorna Earl (2007) has identified three broad categories to encompass this variety of purposes: assessment *of* learning, assessment *for* learning, and assessment *as* learning.

Assessment *of* learning is used to compare individual student performance to what other students can do and to assign a grade to that performance. It is what we think of most often when we think of assessment. Although this type of assessment is an important and necessary component of instruction, it is by no means the primary reason for conducting assessment. Assessment *for* learning is formative assessment, carried out to reveal student progress toward a goal. Instructors use this type of assessment to identify students' strengths and weaknesses and to adjust teaching strategies accordingly. Finally, assessment *as* learning takes place when students use information from an assessment to moderate their own study strategies. This powerful form of assessment is extremely important for online students in helping them develop skills as self-regulated learners. Such skills include managing time, setting goals, reflecting on one's own work, assessing progress, and applying appropriate strategies (Zimmerman 2002). Students who develop these skills are able to seek help when necessary, regulate their motivation, persist in task completion, and appropriately attribute success to their efforts.

A final recommendation encompasses all the key recommendations from the previous section: whenever possible, aim for assessment *as* learning. Assessments designed for this purpose make optimal use of the instructor's effort in designing and grading the assessment as well as provide the best opportunity for students to enrich their learning and mature as lifelong learners.

FURTHER READING

"Assessment/Evaluation Topics: Assessing Learning Objectives Bloom's Taxonomy." Illinois Online Network. Accessed May 27, 2011. http://www.ion.uillinois.edu/resources/tutorials/assessment/bloomtaxonomy.asp. This one-page refresher outlines learning objectives for use in creating assessments aligned with levels of Bloom's Taxonomy.

"Australian Flexible Learning Quick Guide Series: Assessment and Online Teaching." 2002. Australian Flexible Learning Framework. Accessed May 27, 2011. http://pre2005.flexible-learning.net.au/guides/assessment.pdf. This quick guide provides a short introduction to assessment for online learning. It covers common issues faced by online instructors in making assessment decisions and offers examples of assessments for use in online environments.

Palloff, Rena M., and Keith Pratt. 2009. *Assessing the Online Learner: Resources and Strategies for Faculty*. San Francisco, CA: John Wiley and Sons. For those seeking a more comprehensive resource, this book can be used by both beginning and experienced online instructors to inform the design of online assessments. In addition to reliable coverage of important issues in assessment of online learners, it includes many examples of assessments from a variety of college-level and professional development online courses.

Simonson, Michael, Sharon Smaldino, Michael Albright, and Susan Zvacek. 2002. "Assessment for Distance Education." In *Teaching and Learning at a Distance: Foundation of Distance Education* (2nd ed., pp. 492–541). Columbus, OH: Prentice-Hall. Accessed May 25, 2011. http://www.nova.edu/~simsmich/pdf/entire.pdf. Although it is the third edition that has been cited throughout the chapter, the second edition of this book is available online and so offers an accessible resource. Its chapter on assessment covers purposes of assessment, general assessment principles, and explanations of traditional and alternative assessment methods for online learning.

REFERENCES

"Assessment and Online Teaching." 2002. Australian Flexible Learning Framework. Accessed May 5, 2011. http://www.flexiblelearning.net.au/guides/assessment.pdf.

Arend, Bridget D. 2007. "Course Assessment Practices and Student Learning Strategies in Online Courses." *Journal of Asynchronous Learning Networks* 11 (4): 3–13.

Baron, Julie, and Steven M. Crooks. 2005. "Academic Integrity in Web Based Distance Education." *TechTrends* 49 (2): 40–45.

Black, Paul, and Dylan Wiliam. 1998. "Inside the Black Box: Raising Standards through Classroom Assessment." *Phi Delta Kappan* 80 (2): 139–148.

Bloom, Benjamin S. 1987. *Taxonomy of Educational Objectives. Book 1: Cognitive Domain.* New York, NY: Longman.

Bloxham, Sue, and Pete Boyd. 2007. *Developing Effective Assessment in Higher Education: A Practical Guide.* New York, NY: Open University Press.

Booth, Robin, Berwyn Clayton, Robert Hartcher, Susan Hungar, Patricia Hyde, and Penny Wilson. 2003. *The Development of Quality Online Assessment in Vocational Education and Training: Volume 1.* Kensington Park, SA, Australia: Australian National Training Authority. Accessed June 2, 2011. http://www.ncver.edu.au/publications/962.html.

Burton, Steven J., Richard R. Sudweeks, Paul F. Merrill, and Bud Wood. 1991. *How to Prepare Better Multiple-Choice Test Items: Guidelines for University Faculty.* Provo, UT: Brigham Young University Testing Services. Accessed June 3, 2011. http://testing.byu.edu/info/handbooks/betteritems.pdf.

Cohen, Alan S. 1987. "Instructional Alignment: Searching for a Magic Bullet." *Educational Researcher* 16: 16–20.

Dikli, Semire. 2003. "Assessment at a Distance: Traditional vs. Alternative Assessments." *Turkish Online Journal of Educational Technology* 2 (3). Accessed June 3, 2011. http://www.tojet.net/articles/v2i3/232.pdf.

Earl, Lorna M. 2007. "Assessment as Learning." In *The Keys to Effective Schools: Educational Reform as Continuous Improvement* (2nd ed.), edited by Willis D. Hawley, 85–98. Thousand Oaks, CA: Corwin Press.

Gaytan, Jorge, and Beryl C. McEwen. 2007. "Effective Online Instructional and Assessment Strategies." *American Journal of Distance Education* 21 (3): 117–32.

Gibbs, Graham, and Claire Simpson. 2004–5. "Conditions under Which Assessment Supports Students' Learning." *Learning and Teaching in Higher Education* 1: 3–31. Accessed May 25, 2011. http://www2.glos.ac.uk/offload/tli/lets/lathe/issue1/articles/simpson.pdf.

Grijalva, Therese C., Joe Kerkvliet, and Clifford Nowell. 2006. "Academic Honesty and Online Courses." *College Student Journal* 40 (1): 180–85.

Haladyna, Thomas M. 1994. *Developing and Validating Multiple-Choice Test Items.* Hillsdale, NJ: Lawrence Erlbaum Associates.

Hannafin, Michael, Kevin Oliver, Janette R. Hill, Evan Glazer, and Priya Sharma. 2003. "Cognitive and Learning Factors in Web-Based Distance Learning Environments." In *Handbook of Distance Education*, edited by Michael Grahame Moore and William G. Anderson, 245–260. Mahwah, NJ: Lawrence Erlbaum Associates.

Harmon, Oskar R., and James Lambrinos. 2008. "Are Online Exams an Invitation to Cheat?" *Journal of Economic Education* 39 (2): 116–25.

Kennedy, Kristen, Sheri Nowak, Renuka Raghuraman, Jennifer Thomas, and Stephen F. Davis. 2000. "Academic Dishonesty and Distance Learning: Student and Faculty Views." *College Student Journal* 34 (2): 309–14.

Kim, Nari, Matthew J. Smith, and Kyungeun Maeng. 2008. "Assessment in Online Distance Education: A Comparison of Three Online Programs at a University." *Online Journal of Distance Learning Administration* 11 (1). Accessed June 2, 2011. http://www.westga.edu/~distance/ojdla/spring111/kim111.html.

Lamb, Brian. 2004. "Wide Open Spaces: Wikis, Ready or Not." *EDUCAUSE Review* (September/October). Accessed May 27, 2011. http://www.educause.edu/ir/library/pdf/ERM0452.pdf.

Levy, Yair. 2007. "Comparing Dropouts and Persistence in E-learning Courses." *Computers and Education* 48: 185–204.

Liang, Xin, and Kim Creasy. 2004. "Classroom Assessment in Web-Based Instructional Environment: Instructors' Experience." *Practical Assessment, Research and Evaluation* 9, (7). Accessed June 1, 2011. http://PAREonline.net/getvn.asp?v=9&n=7.

McAlpine, Mhairi. 2002. "Principles of Assessment." Computer Assisted Assessment Centre. Accessed June 3, 2011. http://www.caacentre.ac.uk/dldocs/Bluepaper1.pdf.

Piezon, Sherry L., and Robin L. Donaldson. 2005. "Online Groups and Social Loafing: Understanding Student-Group Interactions." *Online Journal of Distance Learning Administration* 8 (4). Accessed May 27, 2011. http://www.westga.edu/~distance/ojdla/winter84/piezon84.htm.

Robles, Marcel, and Sandy Braathen. 2002. "Online Assessment Techniques." *The Delta Pi Epsilon Journal* 44 (1): 39–49.

Rovai, Alfred P. 2000. "Online and Traditional Assessments: What Is the Difference?" *Internet and Higher Education* 3: 141–51.

Sadler, D. Royce. 1989. "Formative Assessment and the Design of Instructional Systems." *Instructional Science* 18: 119–44.

Scriven, Michael. 1991. *Evaluation Thesaurus* (4th ed.). Newbury Park, CA: SAGE Publications.

Seale, Jane K., Judith Chapman, and Christine Davey. 2000. "The Influence of Assessments on Students' Motivation to Learn in a Therapy Degree Course." *Medication Education* 34 (6): 614–21.

Simonson, Michael, Sharon Smaldino, Michael Albright, and Susan Zvacek. 2006. *Teaching and Learning at a Distance: Foundation of Distance Education* (3rd ed.). Upper Saddle River, NJ: Pearson Education.

Snyder, Benson R. 1971. *The Hidden Curriculum.* New York, NY: Alfred A Knopf.

Swan, Karen. 2001. "Virtual Interaction: Design Factors Affecting Student Satisfaction and Perceived Learning in Asynchronous Online Courses." *Distance Education* 22 (2): 306–31.

Vandehay, Michael A., George M. Diekhoff, and Emily E. LaBeff. 2007. "College Cheating: A Twenty-Year Follow-Up and the Addition of an Honor Code." *Journal of College Student Development* 48 (4): 468–80.

Wiggins, Grant, and Jay McTighe. 1998. *Understanding by Design.* Alexandria, VA: Association for Supervision and Curriculum Development.

Zimmerman, Barry J. 2002. "Becoming a Self-Regulated Learner: An Overview." *Theory into Practice* 41 (2): 65–70.

5

Overview, Best Practices, and Literature Review

Arianne Hartsell-Gundy and Beth Tumbleson

Online learning rests on the efforts of pioneers in education who have overcome barriers of distance, time, and access. Making education available to students is not a new endeavor; rather, it is an evolving one. Librarians have always played a role in lifelong learning as they have stored, classified, and circulated materials and provided reference assistance to patrons. Twenty-first century librarians are now cast in the role of educator, information specialist, instructional designer, and information technologist to advance online learning. Whether creating online learning modules or supporting faculty and students within Learning management systems, librarians link end users to essential electronic resources and library services. This chapter will provide a brief overview of online learning for beginning distance learning librarians or instruction librarians seeking to engage students in their online learning spaces. It will also introduce best practices for designing online modules and embedded librarianship within the learning management system or collaborative learning environment. Finally, it will supply a current annotated bibliography of books, websites, and journals of professional organizations that librarians can consult to expand their understanding of the tools and techniques needed to work effectively in this newest method of delivering information literacy instruction.

DISTANCE EDUCATION LANDMARKS

In the 1800s, distance learning was launched via correspondence courses in Europe and the United States. Materials were mailed to students using the postal system. Early in the 1900s through the 1930s, educators turned to radio and television to provide instructional content. In 1967 President Johnson authorized the Corporation for Public Broadcasting, which enabled television and radio to be used for noncommercial purposes, such as education. In 1969 the British Open University began granting degrees as a distance-learning institution utilizing radio, television, and computer software. In the 1980s and 1990s, distance learning began to rely on satellite TV and the Internet. In 1987 community colleges and universities began using cable networks to offer courses and degree programs, as exemplified by the creation of the Mind Extension University. In 1989 the University of Phoenix first offered its online degree programs, and in 1997 the California Virtual University began operations.[1] Through the centuries, learning has relied on emerging technologies; educators have adapted by incorporating the latest delivery mechanisms into their instruction.

ONLINE LEARNING

Online learning has become an accepted method of education and training in the United States. Indeed, it is revolutionizing access to degrees, programs, and training. Educators in such varied environments as K–12, higher education, the military, and corporations now provide web-based distance-learning programs. According to a 2001 *CQ Researcher* report, more than 1,600 out of 5,000 two-year and four-year public and private schools in the United States offered undergraduate and graduate degrees on the Internet in 1999. According to the U.S. Department of Education, 54,000 Internet-based academic courses were offered to 1.6 million enrolled students in 1998.[2] A *Chronicle of Higher Education* article published in 2010 noted that online-only enrollment is anticipated to reach 3.97 million students by 2014 ("Online Learning"). According to the Instructional Technology Council's *2010 Distance Education Survey Results* (2011), criminal justice, computer and information technology, healthcare, business, nursing, public administration, liberal arts, communication, education, and psychology comprise the ten fields that constitute 81 percent of all online enrollment. The University of Phoenix Online, a for-profit institution, enrolls the largest number of students, at 400,000.[3] In 2001 the education and workforce training market—$815 billion per year—was second only to health care in the United States.[4]

Online learning appeals to those seeking flexible scheduling, whether for reasons of family, job, or other academic commitments. For example, single mothers, who are often part-time returning students, prefer the convenience of online learning. Online learning is accessible to those who cannot commute to an academic campus, such as those living in isolated rural areas, people with disabilities, soldiers on active duty, prison inmates, or would-be-students who live far from an institution offering the desired degree. It also serves the needs of those who cannot afford to commute due to high fuel costs or the potential loss of income because of time spent away from a job. According to Rosenfield, CEO of UNext.com, only "1 percent of the world's 18-year-olds go off to college."[5] Many students today stop formal education temporarily before they start undergraduate or graduate school in favor of "exploratory years." The worldwide demand for US higher education, moreover, may reach 160 million students by 2025 according to a Merrill Lynch report.[6] Also, due to the economic downturn of recent years, construction on campus has been delayed or cancelled, potentially limiting the availability of on-campus opportunities. Consequentlyonline education becomes a viable solution to expand access to higher education.

In the same way that education has undergone rapid and radical change due to market demand and emerging technologies, so has the publishing industry. Academic libraries no longer rely solely on print collections. They now purchase electronic resources and subscribe to numerous online databases of full-text journal articles and books as well as multimedia collections. Still another trend in scholarly research publishing is "open access," wherein an institution or author permits others to benefit from formerly closed collections or content and make them freely available online and able to be reused for scholarly purposes. Yale University now provides open access to the digital images in its cultural heritage collection. (See http:// news.yale.edu/2011/05/10/digital-images-yale-s-vast-cultural-collections-now -available-free.) The Library of Congress has made its National Jukebox of 10,000 historical sound recordings freely available as well. (See http://www.loc.gov/ jukebox.) Amazingly, virtual libraries are open 24/7 to online learners. The happy convergence of learning management systems with electronic resources enables online learners to pursue research via the university library website. Faculty can assign research papers, presentations, and projects, confident that their students have access to authoritative, scholarly resources without having to travel to the physical library. Consequently, distance and instruction librarians are employing new approaches to collaborate with faculty and offer library services to on- and off-campus students.

EMBEDDED LIBRARIANS COLLABORATE WITH FACULTY AND STUDENTS ONLINE

"Online learning" may be defined as distance learning that relies primarily on instruction provided via computers with Internet access. Learning occurs online in a collaborative learning environment, rather than in the face-to-face classroom. Online learning may be either "synchronous," which means all students gather at designated times to chat or receive instruction in real time, or "asynchronous," which means students undertake learning at different times to fit their individual schedules. Embedded librarianship is a new approach to providing information literacy instruction. Through collaboration with faculty members, the embedded librarian places research strategies and links to electronic resources customized to students' research assignments within a course via a learning management system (LMS). Universities and colleges use various systems such as Blackboard, Sakai, Moodle, and Desire2Learn. Embedded librarianship works equally well with traditional, hybrid, and online courses and can be used with upper- and lower-division courses in any discipline. The embedded librarian calls upon standard reference and instructional methods to deliver research assistance to students at their point of need in online spaces already familiar to students. Embedded librarians can use lessons learned from working at the reference desk, one-shot instruction sessions, information literacy credit courses, and the library website in this new online setting to strengthen student learning and achievement. Staffing may need to be realigned to best serve current needs of students who no longer show up at the reference desk or never start their research at the library website, as survey respondents made plain in OCLC's (2011) *Perceptions of Libraries, 2010: Context and Community*.[7] Embedded librarianship is becoming the new norm rather than an innovative method. Indeed, "[e]mbedded librarianship is the primary and most productive method academic librarians have to interact with students and faculty and teach the research process, its rationale, and skills."[8] Librarians need to be designing online learning module content because students are already doing much of their coursework online.

ONLINE LEARNING LITERATURE REVIEW FOR LIBRARIANS

A search of the literature makes it apparent how common the concept of online embedded librarianship has become. A recent search for the terms "online learning" and "librarian" in *Library, Information Science & Technology Abstracts with Full Text* generated more than 150 results. Librarians are writing about many different aspects of online learning, including collaborating with faculty, serving distance learning students, experimenting with social media tools, teaching online information literacy credit courses, and embedding content and services into learning management systems. Recent articles have looked at new tools to enhance online teaching and learning, students' perceptions of online learning, and best practices.

Many librarians are experimenting with new ways to deliver content. Susan E. Montgomery (2010) advocates for using online webinars. She explains that webinars are more interactive than static tutorials using programs like Camtasia, but they also allow for more flexibility because a librarian can potentially schedule several webinars to fit different students' schedules.[9] Amanda Click and Joan Petit (2010) focus on using Web 2.0 social networking tools. They explain why they think these tools are useful for librarians in their conclusion: "The most compelling reasons for libraries to use these technologies, then, are two-fold: our users are already there and may be talking about us; and by using these technologies, we better understand our users and help them become savvier consumers and creators of information."[10] Simone Williams (2010) gives details and advice about a variety of different tools that might be useful for online information literacy instruction, including course management systems, podcasts, screencasts, blogs, web-based games, and virtual three-dimensional environments.[11]

Other librarians are beginning to do research on how effective online environments are for student learning. For example, Karen Anderson and Frances A. May (2010) conducted a field experiment to compare how face-to-face, online, and hybrid learning formats influence students' retention of information literacy skills. The scores on their posttests for measuring retention of information literacy skills showed that there was little difference in students' retention of information literacy among those who took face-to-face, online, or hybrid classes.[12] Lori S. Mestre (2010) explored whether online instructional tools designed by librarians accommodate students with different learning styles. Mestre surveyed librarians and conducted student usability interviews. In her conclusion, Mestre shares significant results: "The results of the study indicate that students recommend the use of multiple modalities in the design of learning objects. They prefer that the learning objects include both images and sound, are visually engaging, and are available at point-of-need, with some way to pick and choose sections to review."[13]

Now that librarians have been involved in online learning for several years, many librarians are beginning to focus on best practices. Starr Hoffman and Lilly Ramin (2010) performed a literature review, used Ramin's case study, and did a mixed methods study of embedded librarianship at six institutions. Their best practices included tips for the following categories: preparing and developing the service, time management, using the course management software, and avoiding technical problems.[14] Amy C. York and Jason M. Vance (2009) did a similar study. They reviewed the professional literature and created an online survey of academic librarians. Among their best practices: (1) Know the campus course management system (CMS) and its administrators. (2) Get a library link in the CMS. (3) Go beyond the library link. (4) Don't become overextended—recruit some help. (5) Be strategic with course selection and time. (6) Be an active participant in the class. (7) Market the embedded librarian service.[15] The tips and best practices outlined below expand upon some of these best practices while also extending into other areas such as academic honesty and copyright.

BEST PRACTICES IN EMBEDDED LIBRARIANSHIP

Collaboration is fundamental to embedded librarianship. The instruction librarian or distance librarian must invite faculty to partner in the LMS for student achievement. It is rare that instructors will initiate the request, as it may seem an imposition on their part and they do not assume it is a standard service that librarians offer. Embedded librarians may build course content relevant to research assignments in a given course. Sometimes the instructor only desires a research guide or links placed within the course at the start of the course. At other times, the faculty member prefers that the embedded librarian show up in the online course for a defined research project period. Still other faculty seek an ongoing collaboration throughout the entire term. Sometimes collaboration involves the embedded librarian's teaching a one-shot information literacy session at the faculty's request. The ideal collaboration is often at the assignment level. In these cases, the embedded librarian may help redesign an instructor's research assignment. For instance, in a public health nursing assignment, the embedded librarian suggested that the biographical research be expanded to compare past public health nurse reformers with present-day nurses using a database new to the nurse educator, *Biography in Context*. This collaboration resulted in a more meaningful project for students. As the partnership continues from semester to semester, trust develops and further research assignment redesign may ensue.

Communication is essential to effective embedded librarianship. In an effort to support the instructor and reach enrolled students in the LMS course, embedded librarians employ various communication channels: IM widgets, texting, e-mail, telephone, and office appointments. Be sure to indicate the hours and days you are available to students so they have realistic expectations of when they may reach the embedded librarian. No one lives online 24/7; everyone unplugs. You might even indicate which communication method(s) you favor and which will offer students the fastest response. Within the course, the embedded librarian may choose to communicate with all users using the LMS e-mail tool or announcements tool or by creating and replying to the Ask-a-Librarian thread in the discussion board. Some students may also be interested in making a research consultation appointment, if they understand that option is available. Timely communication is needed to reach students at their point of need. Instructors should give serious thought to scaffolding semester projects into smaller assignments with multiple deadlines. This gets students who tend to procrastinate to begin working. Assign deadlines for a developed topic and single research question, keywords and subject terms being used in searching, named research databases, reference collections and other information sources, or an annotated bibliography. It is very important for the embedded librarian to note these assignment deadlines, place them in an Outlook calendar or the like, and send out research tips one to two weeks prior to the due date, when students are likely to be most receptive to research strategies and suggestions. E-mail, send an announcement, or post to a discussion board thread a just-in-time recommendation of several electronic resources or a research tip. In this way, the embedded librarian gains the attention of students who may be stuck, confused, or frustrated.

Content comprises the guts of embedded librarianship. Online students must be able to find and use the electronic resources and strategies relevant to the course-related research assignments. Often students seek a shortcut through the overwhelming options available online. They may not distinguish between the free web and the fee-based resources that libraries subscribe to and purchase. If links to authoritative electronic resources are obvious and limited to the most relevant, then students are likely to click and search for needed information rather than fall back on old coping strategies using the familiar Google and Wikipedia. Locating library links to resources next to the assignment is best. They may also be placed on a separate embedded librarian page, which collects all research help in one place. Materials that should be promoted include research databases, e-book collections, electronic journals, authoritative web-sites and portals, library consortia, online catalogs, digital media, LibGuides (subject-specific interactive research guides), screencasts, and citation tools. By steering students and simplifying choices, librarians can introduce students to the standard research titles, collections, and databases in a given field, whether it be English or engineering.

Research concepts are important skills that librarians need to teach. All students are increasingly dependent on using online tools to find information sources for research papers and projects, but this is especially true for online learners who may not have access to a physical library. As a result, it's even more important to help students learn to think critically about finding, evaluating, and using information. The ACRL Information Literacy Competency Standards for Higher Education (http://www.ala.org/ala/mgrps/divs/acrl/standards/informationliteracycompetency.cfm) should be carefully considered when creating learning objects and lesson plans to help online students. Research topics to consider might include how to develop a research topic and question, how to search for information in research databases, how to evaluate websites, how to use sources to support arguments, how to cite sources, and how to comply with copyright rules. Embedded librarians need to think carefully about effectively teaching such concepts online. The chosen method may depend on the nature of the concept to be taught, the discipline, and the needs of students and instructors. Librarians should move beyond posting a subject guide handout or creating a learning management system page. Creative alternatives might include making a short video that outlines copyright rules and fair use, building a tutorial using software like Camtasia to demonstrate how to craft search terms, or chatting online in Blackboard Collaborate with small groups of students to answer their specific questions and give timely research guidance. Creativity is an important component in keeping students' attention and helping them understand the research process better.

Online writing is intended for online readers, who behave very differently from deep readers. Few speed-read *Plato's Republic* and come away with profound insights. Online readers spend less time with text. Online reading often involves skimming content quickly; therefore, formatting plays a starring role. Using headings and bulleted lists, placing important material at the top of the page, writing with concise language rather than words-a-plenty, and using plain, easily understood words are all hallmarks of online writing. Although course creators think everything included in the modules is important, not all text can be in bold or color or a large font. Give careful consideration to marking text in these ways; less is best. The embedded librarians who keep these guidelines in mind connect with users.

Academic honesty is a value upheld in education from elementary through graduate school. Those designing online learning modules do well to structure assessments in such a way as to strengthen the likelihood of student compliance with institutional academic integrity requirements. Assignments that include unique elements only found in course readings and lectures necessitate original work. Requiring submissions at various stages of a research project provides evidence of a student's individual progress. Instructing students in how to cite sources according to specific citation styles may prevent instances of plagiarism. Using anti-plagiarism tools such as Turnitin.com for electronic submissions is another means of teaching academic honesty and holding students accountable to write unique essays. Students should understand that their paper will be run against a vast database of web content and previously submitted work and that any matching text will be reported in an originality report. Some instructors choose to hold final exams in traditional classrooms where students are proctored. In other cases, online students are required to take the online test at local college libraries after showing identification. In this way, it is possible for library staff to proctor the exam in progress on a library computer.

Copyright is another extremely important consideration for those designing online modules. Instructors often have questions about whether they may use publications and media in their online courses. For that matter, so do librarians. John Burke (2011) clarifies key concepts in his "Audiovisual Conundrums" presentation.[16] Librarians are neither attorneys nor law enforcement officers. The copyright landscape is ever changing, as headlines attest. Publishers and authors are rewriting policy as they deliver more electronic and digital content. In designing online modules, do link to digital videos at sites such as YouTube or iTunesU. Use shared learning objects like MERLOT. Make use of images offered under Creative Commons license, as at Flickr (http://www.flickr .com/). Use music in the public domain, such as the Library of Congress's National Jukebox, or royalty-free music at websites such as http://incompetech.com/. Course builders may link to, download, or stream media and media collections provided by their university library or library consortium. In this way, online students may learn how to manipulate media messages, analyze content, or remix and transform media, and thereby develop media literacy. Fair Use (Section 107) and the Teach Act (Sections 110 and 112) of Title 17 of the U.S. Code permit usage of copyrighted content in online classroom, just as in face-to-face classroom settings, by accredited, nonprofit institutions during limited class time by registered course students.

Technology plays a tremendous role in successfully delivering online learning. It is advisable to link to the exact section of interest rather than to a website's homepage. Links to electronic resources and tools should be named, so students know where clicking a link will lead. Links should be easy to notice via color, font, or size. Links should be checked on- and off-campus to make sure that connections to images, text, and videos work. If a proxy server address is needed as part of the authentication process, add it. If a resource or site needs to open in a new window to load properly, be sure to select that option. It is also recommended that content posted in online modules be checked using different browsers, such as Safari, Internet Explorer, Mozilla Firefox, and Chrome, and different screen resolutions to make sure that content displays properly. Images should include captions. Documents should be published in PDF files so that they will be readable by every student and will not require commercial software, such as a Microsoft application. Another advantage of PDF files is that content is safeguarded, as it cannot be altered. Embed links to digital videos as needed.

Create digital videos or screencasts as needed to provide 24/7 instruction in searching databases and catalogs or explaining aspects of the research process. Explore and use open-source products such as Jing, or commercial products such as Camtasia or Adobe Captivate to create screencasts of your own. These kinds of software can allow for digital videos, narrated slide shows, screenshots, closed captioning, and quizzes. Create a screencast on citing sources or conducting a literature review as part of an online module. If preferred, use ready-made tutorials available at PRIMO (Peer-Reviewed Instructional Materials Online Database) or ANTS (Animated Tutorial Sharing). Consider interacting with students synchronously using webinar software such as Blackboard Collaborate or Adobe Connect. Such sessions can be recorded and then used asynchronously.

Become informed about accessibility issues. Make online learning module content accessible to those who may be color-blind or have impaired vision, hearing, mobility, or motor skills. In his article "Equality through Access," Christopher Guder (2010) encourages librarians to become knowledgeable about Americans with Disabilities Act standards and web accessibility standards. He urges librarians to contact their institution's office of disabilities services. Adaptive technology software can now be loaded on flash drives so that students do not need to work at designated computers. Such technical issues will enhance online learning—or hinder it, if ignored. Sometimes partnering with instructional designers, information technologists, webmasters, or campus offices will improve the learning experience for all online students. Do not hesitate to seek additional technical expertise when needed.

Finally, the **human factor** cannot be overlooked or minimized as one works in online learning. Online embedded librarians are most effective when they are proactive, perseverant, and patient as they collaborate with faculty and students and work through curricular or technical difficulties that inevitably arise. Time is needed to establish trust between the embedded librarian and faculty and their students. Being curious and creative is necessary to build meaningful content and enter into the research dilemmas that students encounter. Having a sense of humor and optimism defuses techno-stress that surfaces when online connections fail or users do not know how to proceed. If an embedded librarian is an extrovert, empathetic, and experienced, then online users will eventually respond. Making inroads into educational cultures not used to collaborating for student success is a worthy mission and returns satisfying dividends.

ANNOTATED BIBLIOGRAPHY

This bibliography is a collection of books, journals, and websites to help you become informed about current online learning practices. It is in no way complete but rather is meant to be a brief collection of practical resources, particularly for academic librarians. Some of these resources are specific to libraries, but others explore online learning more generally to give librarians context and a more complete picture.

Books

Anglin, Gary J. 2011. *Instructional Technology: Past, Present, and Future* (3rd ed.). Santa Barbara, California: Libraries Unlimited.

Instructional Technology is now in its third edition and is edited by Gary J. Anglin, program coordinator of the Instructional Design Program at the University of Kentucky. Though the intended audience is graduate students, anyone wanting a good overview of instructional technology would find this book useful because it gives a good background on the important issues in the field. The diverse contributors—many are well-known instructional designers—give an excellent overview of the subject, including history, critical issues, instructional development, and research and theory. Every chapter includes notes and references. This third edition includes some new material, so it may be useful to look at the earlier editions for a more comprehensive picture of the field.

Bell, Steven J., and John D. Shank. 2007. *Academic Librarianship by Design: A Blended Librarian's Guide to the Tools and Techniques*. Chicago: American Library Association.

This book is a must for librarians interested in online learning because it focuses on instructional design and technology for librarians. In fact, the definition of blended librarianship is this precise combination of skills. The book presents BLAAM (Blended Librarians' Adapted ADDIE Model)—adopted from the instructional systems design ADDIE—as a philosophy that librarians can use to guide development of instructional tools and services. It includes scenarios, case studies, profiles of blended librarians, and information about other great resources. Though the whole book is useful, the chapters focusing on applying blended librarianship to information literacy through course management systems and digital learning materials are particularly interesting. Steven J. Bell is the associate university librarian for research and instructional services at Temple University, and John D. Shank is the instructional design librarian and the director for learning technologies at the Berks campus of Pennsylvania State University. They are also the cofounders of the Blended Librarians Online Learning Community on the LearningTimes Network. See the Blended Librarian Portal at http://www.blendedlibrarian.org/index.html.

Benson, Robyn. 2010. *Online Learning and Assessment in Higher Education: A Planning Guide*. Oxford: Chandos Publishing.

This practical guide for instructors was written by senior lecturers in educational design and e-learning at Monash University in Australia. It focuses on helping an instructor plan how to succeed in online learning, so it includes chapters on topics such as choosing the best tools, thinking about how students learn, designing and developing online learning environments, and planning for assessment. Each chapter includes helpful tables and real-world examples. The conclusion includes a checklist to help instructors think carefully about their courses. This checklist requires instructors to answer yes, no, or unsure to such questions as "Are you able to identify the kinds of specific learning resources and supports that you will need to design for the activities you plan to develop?"

Mackey, Thomas P., and Trudi Jacobson. 2008. *Using Technology to Teach Information Literacy*. New York: Neal-Schuman Publishers.

This book focuses on using technology to help teach information literacy skills in a variety of contexts. Though it includes the use of technology in both face-to-face classroom environments and online learning, most of what is covered will be of interest to librarians teaching information literacy and research skills in online environments. The book is divided into three parts. The first part examines using the web for collaboration and outlines several faculty-librarian partnerships. The second part explores using course management systems to encourage active learning. The third part focuses on online assessment. Each chapter includes useful information such as literature reviews, institutional backgrounds, disciplinary perspectives, case studies, assessment strategies, and references. The book includes several appendices with sample learning objectives, learning outcomes, survey questions, etc. The contributors include both librarians and professors.

Websites

"ACRL Distance Learning Section." ACRL Distance Learning Section. March 20, 2011. Accessed May 20, 2011. http://caspian.switchinc.org/~distlearn/.

The Association of College and Research Libraries Distance Learning Section is a subgroup within ACRL for librarians who support distance education students. Its website includes information about the group (committees, membership information, volunteer forms) and useful tools for librarians. Tools include the Standards for Distance Learning Library Services, A Guide for New Distance Learning Librarians, distance learning statistics, research, and instructional resources. The website has information about joining the group's listserv (OFF-CAMP) and a wiki. Though their focus is on distance education, many of the resources are relevant to librarians working in an online environment. Some of the information is a little out of date, but much of it is still relevant.

"AACE—Association for the Advancement of Computing in Education." Association for the Advancement of Computing in Education. 2011. Accessed May 20, 2011. http://www.aace.org/.

The Association for the Advancement of Computing in Education is an international organization founded in 1981. According to its website, its mission is to advance "Information Technology in Education and E-Learning research, development, learning, and its practical application." The organization holds international conferences and produces several peer-reviewed publications. In addition to information about the organization and support for members (career center and information about publications), the website includes a digital library. Some of the content available in the digital library is only available with a subscription, though the abstracts are freely accessible. Some content, such as the "Talks," can be viewed without a subscription. These talks include slides and videos from recent conferences. Librarians interested in online learning may be find some of these resources useful because they show the concerns and needs of online instructors. The website provides opportunities for networking, with links to the organization's blog, Ning community, Facebook page, and Twitter account.

"Instructional Technology Council." Instructional Technology Council. 2011. Accessed May 20, 2011. http://www.itcnetwork.org/.

The Instructional Technology Council is an affiliated council of the American Association of Community Colleges that was formed in 1977. As the organization's website explains, it is "working to raise awareness about the benefits of distance learning, instructional telecommunications, and future needs and possibilities." It provides conferences, online webinars, leadership academies, reports, and forums for members. On the website you can find resources like abstracts for the organization's journals, information about grant opportunities, student resources, legislative actions, and newsletter articles. See especially the Council's most recent report, *The 2010 Distance Education Survey Results: Trends in eLearning: Tracking the Impact of eLearning at Community Colleges*, for valuable information.

"Off-Campus Library Services." Central Michigan University Off-Campus Library Services. May 02, 2011. Accessed May 24, 2011. http://ocls.cmich.edu/.

Central Michigan University is a leader in library services for distance learning. Librarians will find it useful to look at its website to see an example of how to organize resources and information for distance education students. Resources for students include research guides, sample projects, documents on demand, and research assistance. Central Michigan University also plans the biannual Distance Library Services Conference, so you can find a link to conference information from the website. At this international conference, librarians, administrators, and educators from both nonprofit and for-profit institutions discuss, demonstrate, and champion the techniques and theories of providing library services to students and faculty participating in instruction either away from a main campus or in the online environment.

"What Is EDUCAUSE?" EDUCAUSE. 2011. Accessed May 20, 2011. http://www.educause.edu/. As its website says, "EDUCAUSE is a nonprofit association whose mission is to advance higher education by promoting the intelligent use of information technology." The site includes a wealth of information for instructors and librarians, including professional development resources, applied research, policy advocacy, teaching and learning initiatives, and a variety of publications. There are reports, kits, podcasts, and journal publications, which are archived and available. One report of special interest is the organization's *Horizon Report*, which is published every year and describes six areas of emerging technology that will have significant impact on higher education and creative expression over the next one to five years. Librarians can use these reports to prepare for the needs of online instructors and students.

Journals

Journal of Computer Assisted Learning. Blackwell Publishing Ltd. ISSN: 0266-4909
 This journal is peer reviewed and is published six times a year. It covers the use of information and communication technology to support learning. It's indexed in a variety of databases, including *Academic Search Complete, Computers & Applied Sciences Complete, Education Research Complete, Scopus, ERIC,* and *Web of Science.* Common topics include collaborative learning, knowledge engineering, distance and networked learning, developmental psychology, and evaluation. Librarians will benefit from reading this journal because of the diversity of topics related to computer-assisted learning that are covered.

Journal of Interactive Instruction Development. Society for Applied Learning Technology. ISSN: 1040-0370
 This peer-reviewed journal is published four times a year by the Society for Applied Learning Technology. It's a practical journal "devoted to the issues, problems, and applications of applied learning technologies in education, training, and job performance." The audience includes not just educators but also trainers and professionals in business, industry, the military, and academia. It focuses on interactive multimedia instruction. It's indexed in several databases, including *Computers & Applied Sciences Complete* and *Education Research Complete.* Librarians will find the practical nature of many of the articles very useful.

Journal of Interactive Online Learning. National Center for Online Learning Research. ISSN: 1541-4914
 This peer-reviewed journal is published four times a year by the National Center for Online Learning Research. According to its website, it "focuses on providing a venue for manuscripts, critical essays, and reviews that encompass disciplinary and interdisciplinary perspectives in regards to issues related to higher-level learning outcomes." It has an 11 percent acceptance rate and an extensive editorial review board. It's indexed in a variety of places,

including the *Contemporary Science Association*, *Education Research Complete*, and *Scopus*. Recent articles have focused on diverse topics including Second Life, characteristics of successful online instructors, online student evaluations, and student interactions in online discussion forums.

Journal of Library and Information Services in Distance Learning. Taylor and Francis Ltd. ISSN: 1533-290X

This peer-reviewed quarterly journal addresses the concerns and interests of librarians working in distance education. Formerly, the conference proceedings of Off-Campus Library Services were published in the *Journal of Library Administration*, but starting in 2012 they will be published in this journal. Topics covered include collection development strategies, faculty-librarian partnerships or collaborations, embedded librarianship, cutting-edge instruction and reference techniques, document delivery, remote access, and evaluation. Though topics touch upon many services besides instruction, many of the articles do address information literacy and learning and technology, making it an essential journal for any librarian interested in online learning. The journal is indexed in a variety of databases, including *Academic Search Complete*, *Communication Abstracts Online*, *Education Research Complete*, *Library, Information Science & Technology Abstracts (LISTA)*, *Scopus*, and *Inspec*.

Journal of Web Librarianship. Taylor & Francis Ltd. ISSN: 1932-2909

This journal is peer reviewed and is published four times a year. As its website mentions, it covers "all aspects of librarianship as practiced on the World Wide Web, including both existing and emerging roles and activities of information professionals." It covers web services, systems, public services, technical services, special collections, archives, and administration. The diversity of topics means that many of the articles will not be specifically about online learning. Still, there are a lot of articles on the subject. For example, recent articles have looked at information competency requirements for undergraduates, learning in course management systems, information literacy classes, customizing Blackboard, etc. It's indexed in several databases, including *Library and Information Science and Technology Abstracts (LISTA)* and *Scopus*.

NOTES

1. Brian Hansen, "Distance Learning," *CQ Researcher,* 11, no. 42 (December 2001), http://library.cqpress.com/cqresearcher/cqresrre2001120700 (accessed May 12, 2011): 993–1016.

2. Ibid.

3. 2010. "Online Learning: By the Numbers," *Chronicle of Higher Education,* 57, no. 11 (2010), *Professional Development Collection*, EBSCO *host* 55245101 (accessed May 18, 2011): B28–29.

4. Hansen, "Distance Learning."

5. Ibid.

6. Ibid.

7. Online Computer Library Center, Inc., *OCLC Perceptions of Libraries, 2010: Context and Community* (Dublin, OH: OCLC, 2011), http://www.oclc.org/reports/2010perceptions/2010perceptions_all.pdf (accessed May 18, 2011).

8. John Burke and Beth Tumbleson, "A Declaration of Embeddedness: Instructional Synergies and Sustaining Practices in LMS Embedded Librarianship," *ACRL 2011 Conference Papers*, Chicago, IL: Association of College and Research Libraries (2011), http://www.ala.org/ala/mgrps/divs/acrl/events/national/2011/papers/declaration_embedded.pdf (accessed May 18, 2011): 92.

9. Susan E. Montgomery, "Online Webinars! Interactive Learning Where Our Users Are: The Future of Embedded Librarianship," *Public Services Quarterly* 6, no. 2/3 (2010), *Library, Information Science & Technology Abstracts with Full Text*, EBSCO*host* (accessed May 23, 2011): 306–11.

10. Amanda Click and Joan Petit, "Social Networking and Web 2.0 in Information Literacy," *International Information & Library Review* 42, no. 2 (2010), *Library, Information Science & Technology Abstracts with Full Text*, EBSCO *host* (accessed May 23, 2011): 142.

11. Simone Williams, "New Tools for Online Information Literacy Instruction," *Reference Librarian* 51, no. 2 (2010), *Library, Information Science & Technology Abstracts with Full Text*, EBSCO *host* (accessed May 23, 2011): 148–62.

12. Karen Anderson and Frances A. May, "Does the Method of Instruction Matter? an Experimental Examination of Information Literacy Instruction in the Online, Blended, and Face-to-Face Classrooms," *Journal of Academic Librarianship* 36, no.6, (November 2010): 495–500.

13. Lori S. Mestre, "Matching Up Learning Styles with Learning Objects: What's Effective?," *Journal of Library Administration* 50, no. 7 (October 2010): 808–29.

14. Starr Hoffman and Lilly Ramin, "Best Practices for Librarians Embedded in Online Courses," *Public Services Quarterly* 6, no. 2/3 (2010), *Library, Information Science & Technology Abstracts with Full Text*, EBSCO *host* (accessed May 23, 2011): 292–305.

15. Amy C. York and Jason M. Vance, "Taking Library Instruction into the Online Classroom: Best Practices for Embedded Librarians," *Journal of Library Administration* 49, no. 1/2 (2009), *Library, Information Science & Technology Abstracts with Full Text*, EBSCO *host* (accessed May 23, 2011): 197–209.

16. John Burke, "Audiovisual Conundrums: Legality vs. Equality with Media Resources" (presentation, Spring Workshop of the Distance Learning Interest Group of the Academic Library Association of Ohio, Columbus, OH, May 13, 2011).

REFERENCES

Alters, Sandra, ed. *Colleges and Universities* 2010. "IP Education: Meeting America's Needs?" Detroit: Gale, 2010.

Anderson, Karen, and Frances A. May. 2010. "Does the Method of Instruction Matter? An Experimental Examination of Information Literacy Instruction in the Online, Blended, and Face-to-Face Classrooms." *Journal of Academic Librarianship* 36 (6): 495–500.

Burke, John. 2011. "Audiovisual Conundrums: Legality vs. Equality with Media Resources." Presentation at the spring workshop of the Distance Learning Interest Group of the Academic Library Association of Ohio, Columbus, Ohio, 2011.

Burke, John and Beth Tumbleson. 2011. "A Declaration of Embeddedness: Instructional Synergies and Sustaining Practices in LMS-Embedded librarianship." Paper presented at the biannual conference of the Association of College and Research Libraries, Philadelphia, Pennsylvania, 2011. Accessed May 18, 2011. http://s3.goeshow.com/acrl/national/2011/client_uploads/handouts/declaration_embeddedness.pdf.

Click, Amanda, and Joan Petit. 2010. "Social Networking and Web 2.0 in Information Literacy." *International Information & Library Review* 42 (2): 137–42.

Guder, Christopher. 2010. "Equality through Access: Embedding Library Services for Patrons with Disabilities." *Public Services Quarterly* 6 (2): 315–22.

Hansen, Brian. 2001. "Distance Learning." *CQ Researcher* 11, no. 42. Accessed May 12, 2011. Cqresrre2001120700.

Hoffman, Starr, and Lilly Ramin. 2010. "Best Practices for Librarians Embedded in Online Courses." *Public Services Quarterly* 6 (2): 292–305.

Instructional Technology Council. 2010. "Trends in eLearning: Tracking the Impact of eLearning at Community Colleges." *2010 Distance Education Survey Results*: 1–24. Accessed May 24, 2011. http://www.itcnetwork.org/images/stories/itcannualsurveymay2011final .pdf.

Mestre, Lori S. 2010. "Matching Up Learning Styles with Learning Objects: What's Effective?" *Journal of Library Administration* 50 (7): 808–29.

Montgomery, Susan E. 2010. "Online Webinars! Interactive Learning Where Our Users Are: The Future of Embedded Librarianship."*Public Services Quarterly* 6 (2): 306–11.

Online Computer Library Center, Inc. 2010. "OCLC Perceptions of Libraries, 2010: Context and Community." *OCLC*: 1–58. Accessed May 18, 2011. http://www.oclc.org/reports/ 2010perceptions/2010perceptions_all.pdf.

"Online Learning: By the Numbers." 2010. *Chronicle of Higher Education* 57 (11): B28–29.

Poulin, Russell. 2002. "Distance Learning in Higher Education." In *Encyclopedia of Education*, ed. James W. Guthrie (Vol. 2: Common–Expertise; pp. 589–93). New York: Macmillan Reference USA.

Williams, Simone. 2010. "New Tools for Online Information Literacy Instruction." *Reference Librarian* 51 (2): 148–62.

York, Amy C., and Jason M. Vance. 2009. "Taking Library Instruction into the Online Classroom: Best Practices for Embedded Librarians." *Journal of Library Administration* 49 (1): 197–209.

6

Online Education in Schools

Margaret L. Lincoln

As technology advances continue to transform K–12 schools, online education options are offering alternative choices and venues for teaching and learning. School libraries, long committed to providing physical and intellectual access to instructional materials, are already responding to changing student and teacher needs in the online world. For example, many school libraries that had previously created a virtual presence through a fixed library website now incorporate such Web 2.0 features as blogs and wikis into the library's online space (Richardson 2007). In seeking to define their role in the new realm of virtual learning, school librarians will need to address an essential question. How can an effective infrastructure be established in the online environment so as to support the dynamic and evolving ways that students and teachers use information resources? The involvement of school libraries in the development of online courses suggests a possible means to meet this challenge.

During the academic year 2007–2008, a hybrid or blended online course including face-to-face meetings was piloted at Lakeview High School in Battle Creek, Michigan. The course was created in response to a newly mandated Michigan Department of Education online learning graduation requirement. The curricular focus was information literacy. Blackboard Learning Management System was first used for instruction. Eleventh and twelfth grade students enrolled in the course also gained real-world library work experience. Additionally, various online information literacy activities from the Blackboard course could be incorporated into instructional units taught in other academic departments at Lakeview High School.

Initially determined to have been a successful undertaking, the Introduction to Information Literacy course was offered again to students in 2008–2009, 2009–2010, and 2010–2011. An effort was made through conference presentations and journal articles to share the Lakeview venture into online learning with other school librarians who may be involved in similar projects. The Lakeview experience is one which can be replicated and adapted by other school librarians.

In this chapter, the school library component of this book takes a three-pronged approach to the topic of an online course by considering the **before**, **during**, and **after** phases. In other words, how does one **plan** for, **implement**, and **disseminate** a school library online course?

The **before** phase, or **planning,** needs to be undertaken before setting up a school library online course. The perspective presented here is that of a practitioner, and background information on school libraries and online learning will be provided by means of a short literature review that considers the increase in online learning projects and involvement of school libraries; integration of library and information literacy skills instruction; course content management system options; and librarian/teacher collaborative projects in online learning. It looks at organizational support for school libraries involved in online learning. For example, the work of the International Association for K–12 Online Learning is examined. Information is provided for the Evergreen Education Group, publisher of *Keeping Pace with K–12 Online Learning.* School librarians can find suggestions for engaging in professional development, workshops, and web-based courses so as to better prepare for online learning. One such opportunity is WISE (Web-based Information Science Education). Examples of model courses and best practice are given, including Blackboard's own Exemplary Course Program and successful online course sites associated with New York State's Onondaga-Cortland-Madison Board of Cooperative Educational Services (OCMBOCES) model. Virtual High School Meanderings (the blog of Dr. Michael Barbour of Wayne State University) and Clovis Online School (a blog about an online charter school founded by Dr. Rob Darrow) are highlighted.

In discussing the **during** phase, or how to go about **implementing** a school library online course, a description is given of Lakeview High School and the adherence to state guidelines. A backward design model was followed and course content was developed. Course expectations for library assistants were stipulated. A content management system was selected, and the online course was officially launched. The course underwent evaluation and modifications. An assessment was made as to how effectively information literacy skills were being taught.

The **after** phase covers the process of **disseminating** a school library online course. This phase was accomplished at Lakeview High School by setting up the Regional Education Media Center (REMC) 12 wiki, which provided a collaborative workspace for school librarians and teachers who were interested in online instruction and information literacy skills. The Lakeview online learning experience was shared through offering training to classroom teachers, by engaging in collaborative online projects with colleagues, and by partnering with Wayne State University in a research project. An effort was made to reach out to colleagues on a national level by posting a school library online learning questionnaire on various listservs, by sharing responses and documents, and by calling for action and ongoing involvement of school library professionals in online learning.

Technological advances are propelling us into an exciting but unknown world. As education moves more and more into the virtual realm, the role of school libraries and school librarians is certain to evolve so as to continue to support meaningful teaching and learning.

THE BEGINNINGS OF SCHOOL LIBRARY ONLINE COURSES

Online learning in the K–12 environment has seen sustained, dramatic growth across the nation, with 45 of the 50 states (plus Washington, D.C.) having a state virtual school or online initiative, full-time online schools, or both (Evergreen Group 2009). As a result of different implementation models, a variety of terms have been used to refer to online learning, including *distance education, virtual schooling, e-learning, hybrid courses, asynchronous learning,* and *web-based learning* (Archambault and Crippen 2009).

K–12 online learning is another new field consisting of an estimated $300 million market, which is growing at an estimated pace of 30% annually ("Fast Facts" 2010). The number of K–12 students who engaged in online or blended courses in 2007–2008 is estimated to have been 1,030,000, an increase of 47% over 2005–2006 (Evergreen Group 2009). Michigan became the first state to legislate an online learning requirement for high school students (Armstrong 2007).

Although the increase in online learning projects is well documented in the literature, the involvement of school libraries in this growing trend has been less studied. The September/October 2005 issue of *Knowledge Quest*, however, was devoted to new roles that school librarians are assuming in digital learning environments. In that issue, Abilock (2005) pointed out that students may be considered digital natives and multitaskers but should not learn exclusively from superficial experiences. Students will learn well in real and virtual environments if school librarians participate in the design, development, implementation, support, and assessment of learning. Dando (2005), an early adapter of online course management systems, reported using Blackboard to measure students' information skills during library orientation, to provide students with access to key resources, and to make library announcements. A further function taken on by school librarians in support of online learning is to serve as a mentor to teachers, helping colleagues to acquire the technological and research skills necessary to deliver dynamic and relevant online courses (Rohland-Heinrich and Jensen 2007). School librarians can work with teachers to direct students to discipline-specific, high-quality sources intended to strengthen the virtual learning experience for students.

Several accounts can be found in more recent publications describing the role that school libraries are playing in online learning. The October 2009 issue of *School Library Monthly* points to the use of Moodle (Modular Object-Oriented Dynamic Learning Environment) in an elementary school library setting (Menges 2009). Moodle helped teach the OPAC and served as a forum for the book recommendations of sixth-grade students. Advice for school librarians on how to manage their libraries' online presence is given in the same journal issue. Librarians should select management software, establish levels of access, decide on content, and incorporate such features as discussion groups and survey tools (Fredrick 2009).

The use of Moodle succeeded in permitting a group of some sixty Iowa rural school librarians to stay connected with the modern technology world while participating in a professional development course (Appleton et al. 2009). The class was a combination of face-to-face experiences and distance learning via a statewide fiber-optic network. The class enabled the librarians to begin developing a school library curriculum for the twenty-first century.

As school libraries figure more prominently in the growth of online learning, an instructional focus becomes increasingly apparent. Ensuring that students are effective users of ideas and information is a paramount instructional goal of online courses. The need to teach information literacy and critical thinking skills is consistently emphasized in the educational literature. Schools and academic libraries take on a pivotal role in reinforcing these skills, which are vital to students in an information-overloaded world (Battle 2007). School librarians should actively promote information literacy standards, demonstrating a direct connection to improved education and higher test scores (Yohe 2007).

Research shows that techno-savvy is not synonymous with information-literate. A University of Oklahoma study recommended that information literacy instruction be relevant to students' lives and meshed with their learning styles (Brown, Murphy, and Nanny 2003). Although focused at the college level, this study has applicability for high school curricula in which an attempt is made to include differentiated instruction. A British study also overturns the common assumption that the "Google Generation," youngsters born or brought up in the Internet age, is the most Web-literate. The first ever virtual longitudinal study carried out by the CIBER research team at University College London claims that, although young people demonstrate an apparent ease and familiarity with computers, they rely heavily on search engines, view rather than read, and lack the critical and analytical skills to assess the information that they find on the web (British Library 2008).

School librarians are therefore challenged to effectively integrate information literacy skills into online learning. How can this best be accomplished? According to Esch and Crawford (2006), students should early on be exposed to a university-level online database system with access to both professional and scholarly journals so as to lessen transitional anxiety between high school and college research assignments. Novotny and Cahoy (2006) reported on a usability study that explored how students search the library's online catalog after they have received library instruction. Evidence suggests that instruction tied into students' current research assignment can have a positive effect on user search behaviors and that unnecessary details should be curtailed so as to minimize the boredom factor. Scott and O'Sullivan (2005) studied student search strategies to make a case for integrating information literacy skills into all areas of a school's curriculum, not just in library orientation classes or in isolated skills presentations, so that students can become more skillful at navigating the hypertext environment of the web. By taking advantage of online methods to teach information literacy, librarians can foster self-reliance in students and researchers. Collaborative Web 2.0 tools and rich interactive media—from virtual learning environments to games and Second Life—may be preferred by Generation Y students, who are more geared to looking at images than reading linear text or listening to a lecture (Adolphus 2009).

Improvement in information literacy skills can now even be assessed using TRAILS (Tool for Real-time Assessment of Information Literacy Skills), a freely available online tool created by academic librarians at Kent State University (Schloman and Gedeon 2007). A school librarian can obtain a snapshot of skill levels in order to better tailor instructional efforts. A TRAILS wiki (http://trails-informationliteracy.wikispaces.com/Home+Page/) provides additional assessment support. But while cognitive skills often take precedence in an outcomes-based, standards-driven curriculum, Cahoy (2004) found that the ability to recognize and manage feelings, especially when navigating the research process, is an affective skill that students must master in order to become information-literate. The course structure and logistics of an online class can foster a more personal learning environment in which affective competencies can be addressed.

Once a commitment is made to establish an online course that reinforces information literacy skills, the matter of effective course design and choice of content management system must be considered. A study by Bauer and Kenton (2005) reported that even highly educated and technology-adept teachers are not always able to integrate technology on a consistent basis as a teaching and learning tool. Two key issues were that their students did not have enough time at computers and that teachers needed extra planning time for technology lessons. The use of a content management system in a blended course environment may help to address these identified problems, in that the system can be accessed from school and home by students and by the school librarian. The benefits of the blended or hybrid approach to an online course are also recognized by Tallman and Fitzgerald (2005), who favor the mix of online and face-to-face instruction. Similarly, Kachel, Henry, and Keller (2005) look upon the hybrid online course as the best choice at the high school level, arguing that the format provides extra direction and added motivation needed by secondary school students. These authors emphasize that a good online course must go far beyond a read-this-and-respond correspondence course; instead, it must foster an environment in which students are actively engaged in authentic learning activities. A module, for example, might begin with a video clip or a short scenario of a situation illustrating the module's content. Although online teaching is demanding and time-intensive, adopting to the challenges of using a course content management system can often bring about a renewed excitement for teaching (West, Waddoups, and Graham 2007).

The useful features of Moodle were noted above within the context of the *School Library Monthly* articles. Trotter (2008) discusses Moodle as a free, open-source solution. Moodle's modular design, moreover, enables educators to start incorporating a few tools while working gradually to adapt other online course components. Other teachers have reported success with Moodle as a way to post reading passages and links to websites related to lessons (Tipton 2008). Moodle is seen to have potential as a free web application that educators can use to create effective online learning sites (Guhlin 2009). List and Bryant (2009) used Moodle in an attempt to integrate interactive online content at the middle school level. They found that students were able to engage in an online environment that simulated an authentic online course of the sort they might take in college.

Educational advantages of Blackboard as a content management system are also mentioned in the literature. Jackson (2007) points out that Blackboard may be used to scaffold instruction and infuse information literacy activities throughout subject-specific courses, avoiding one-shot in-person library instruction sessions and instead encouraging students to become lifelong learners. Lang (2007) acknowledges that Blackboard facilitates communication with and among students through e-mail, messaging, and discussion boards; helps an instructor manage paperwork and grading; and provides a convenient place to store and retrieve all course-related documents. According to Pappas (2005), school librarians and classroom teachers can use the discussion board feature of Blackboard in a collaborative way to reinforce information literacy skills, directing students to an organized, threaded arrangement of topics. Giles (2004) writes from the perspective of a college librarian but still shares a useful observation. Involvement in a Blackboard course allows a librarian to interact more extensively with students online rather than simply delivering a stand-alone lecture on finding relevant information sources (2004). An in-depth and favorable analysis of Blackboard as a powerful system for educational instruction, communication, and assessment appeared in the *Journal of Educational Technology Systems* (Bradford et al. 2007). Blackboard's economic success in the market economy (Kowitt 2009) should also not be overlooked.

Finally, it is appropriate to mention an emerging model for higher education with potential applicability to the secondary school setting. In a growing number of institutions, academic librarians are being embedded in online classes through a course content management system. For example, Ramsay and Kinnie (2006) report that at the University of Rhode Island, instead of luring students in, librarians have reached out to distance learners by enrolling as a teaching assistant for online classes. An Embedded Librarian Project is also in place at Daytona Beach College in Florida (Owens 2008). Each semester at Community College of Vermont, faculty members and librarians work together to embed personalized library assistance into online classes (Matthew and Schroeder 2006). An Ask the Librarian Forum might be set up on the Discussion Board or integrated into regular assignments. At Athens State University in Alabama, electronic library assistance is offered to off-site students. A reference librarian is assigned to each class, serving as a teaching assistant and posting announcements, video instructions, and related documents (Herring, Burkhardt, and Wolfe 2009). As they move beyond web pages and online research guides, librarians are becoming true instructional partners in online course management systems (York and Vance 2009).

It is important to consider organizations, exemplary courses, professional development options, and even several blogs that can provide support for school librarians planning to initiate online learning projects. The circumstances surrounding the state of Michigan's online learning requirement served as an impetus for the planning of an online course at Lakeview High School Library.

Organizational Support for School Libraries Involved in Online Learning

A familiarity with existing literature about school libraries involved in online learning will be of help to a school librarian seeking to develop a web-based course, but additional support is available from a variety of organizations. For example, the International Association for K–12 Online Learning is a nonprofit 501(c)(3) membership association based in the Washington, D.C., area. It represents a diverse cross-section of K–12 education, including school districts, charter schools, state education agencies, nonprofit organizations, research institutions, corporate entities, and other content and technology providers. The International Association for K–12 Online Learning website includes sections on research, reports and publications, and promising practices in online learning. *National Standards of Quality for Online Courses* can be downloaded. Presentations including webinars, podcasts, slides and even conference keynote addresses can be accessed. Advocacy document materials are available at http://www.inacol.org/.

The Evergreen Education Group is responsible for issuing and updating the yearly publication *Keeping Pace with K–12 Online Learning: A Review of State-Level Policy and Practice*. This series of annual reports began in 2004 and examines the status of K–12 online education across the country, offering a research-based overview of the latest policies, practices, and trends affecting online learning programs across all 50 states. Sponsor organizations provide critical expertise and guidance in the development and publication of the report. Downloadable files include the full report; year in review; key issues; notes from the field; and state profiles, outlook, and conclusion (http://www.kpk12.com/).

Professional Development, Workshops and Online Courses to Prepare School Librarians for Online Learning

To supplement these organizational resources, a school librarian can prepare for online teaching through professional development, workshops and online courses. Table 6.1 provides summary information for these resources, including active URLs.

Examples of Model Courses and Best Practice

After participating in a professional development offering about online learning pedagogy, it will be helpful to view examples of model online courses and best practice in action. For example, the Blackboard Exemplary Course Program site provides links to award-winning sites and a rubric to assess online courses. Narrated tours with screenshots are available for several courses (http://kb.blackboard.com/display/EXEMPLARY/Exemplary+Course+Program).

Blended Learning in K–12 is a Wikibook created by Norma Scagnoli at the University of Illinois, Urbana-Champaign (http://en.wikibooks.org/wiki/Blended_Learning _in_K-12). The document offers evolution, definitions, types, characteristics, guiding principles, success tips, pedagogical models and references for blended learning.

In New York, the state's Onondaga-Cortland-Madison Board of Cooperative Educational Services (OCMBOCES) aims to develop and provide educational programs and

Table 6.1.
Professional development for online teaching

Resource	Description
Illinois Online Network	**Online Education Resources** includes sections on principles of instructional design, designing an effective course, models and theories, helping others make their courses great, course objectives, and learning styles. http://www.ion.uillinois.edu/resources/tutorials/id/index.asp
University of Wisconsin-Milwaukee	**Teaching & Learning Online** covers learning theory, discussion board, media variety, case studies, simulations, small groups, and learning objects. http://www4.uwm.edu/learningobjects/lo_teach _learn.cfm
Minnesota State Colleges and Universities	**Getting Started Online** is a self-paced tutorial offering readings on key topics, practical tips and suggestions for online teaching, and links to Internet resources for further study. http://ctlstartingonline.project.mnscu.edu/
BestUniversities.com	**How to Create Your Own Online Course: 100 Tools, Guides, and Resources** offers an extensive list of practical tips and how-to guides. http://www.bestuniversities.com/blog/2009/how-to -create-your-own-online-course-100-tools-guides-and-resources/

services of the highest quality. To this end, OCMBOCES has designed a site that allows the visitor to view the way teachers in Central New York have implemented Blackboard as a support environment that connects their classrooms to their students' homes. In recorded webinars, Blackboard users discuss various topics in education and how Blackboard supports their teaching (http://www.blackboard.com/Contact-Us/Events -Center/Webinars-and-Demos/Webinar-Archive.aspx).

The Virtual High School (VHS), a nonprofit organization that offers online credit courses to students across the country and around the world, provides Blackboard demo courses with guest logins. "Day in the Life" is another portion of the VHS site that provides scenarios of what it is like to experience an online course according to the perspectives of a teacher, a student, and a site coordinator (http://www.govhs.org).

It is possible to receive real-time updates about online learning projects through the blogs of educators who are on the cutting edge of this growing phenomenon. Virtual High School Meanderings is written by Dr. Michael Barbour, assistant professor of instructional technology at Wayne State University. Barbour's blog focuses on issues pertaining to distance education within the K–12 system, specifically the use of virtual high schools. Posts can also be accessed through the VHM Newsletter and podcasts (http://virtualschooling.wordpress.com/).

The Clovis Online School serves students from Central California. It is a full-time online school and a free public charter school in California. Clovis opened in August 2009 for ninth and tenth graders and expects to expand to eleventh and twelfth grades in future years. Courses include English, math, social studies, science, foreign languages, physical education, and electives (art history, photography, and graphic design). The Clovis experience is being documented by Principal Dr. Rob Darrow through the Clovis Online School Blog (http://clovisonlineschool.wordpress.com/).

One State's Online Learning Requirement

In Michigan, under the collaborative leadership of former Governor Jennifer M. Granholm, the state board of education, and the state legislature, landmark state graduation requirements have been implemented to give Michigan students the knowledge and skills to succeed in the 21st century and drive the state's economic success in the global economy. One of the requirements is that, beginning with the graduating class of 2011, all high school students will have had a successful online learning experience (Michigan Department of Education 2006). The new Michigan Merit Curriculum also makes it mandatory for high school graduates to have earned 16 academic credits, including four credits each in mathematics and English language arts. For the class of 2016, two credits in world languages are required.

The rationale behind the online learning requirement is that the experience will prepare students for the demands they will encounter in higher education, in the workplace, and in personal lifelong learning. While students informally develop technology skills and gain experience through their media-rich lives, an online learning experience will require them to complete assignments, meet deadlines, learn appropriate online behavior, and effectively collaborate with others in an instructional setting. Michigan's online learning requirement is consistent with one of the core recommendations contained in the previous U.S. Department of Education's National Education Technology Plan, which stipulates that schools should provide every student access to e-learning (U.S. Department of Education 2004). The draft of the National Education

Technology Plan 2010 similarly makes numerous references to online learning (U.S. Department of Education 2010).

In spite of Michigan's current difficult economic picture, the online learning graduation requirement is being implemented. Local school districts have been aided in their efforts to plan for integration of online learning through the support of the Michigan Department of Education and other statewide initiatives. For example, the organization of statewide REMCs has developed several important projects. One REMC-backed project, GenNET Online Learning, offers online courses to secondary school students from accredited providers (http://gennetonline.geneseeisd.org/). Another REMC project grant, Michigan Learns Online, has allowed a web portal to be built addressing the need to expand online instruction throughout the State of Michigan (http://www.remc.org/resources/mlo/). The portal houses learning resources for educators and students and is providing delivery of highly requested student courses. The portal is supporting professional development necessary to ensure that teachers and administrators have the skills necessary to prepare students for success in the twenty-first century.

Michigan Virtual High School, a division of Michigan Virtual University, offers over 150 online courses available to students throughout the state and has created the Career-Forward[1] course in partnership with the Michigan Department of Education and Microsoft Corporation (http://www.mivhs.org/Careers/CareerForward/tabid/273/Default. aspx). The course has helped Michigan students understand how to plan for their work lives and career opportunities amid the implications of the global economy and to satisfy the Michigan Merit Curriculum online.

IMPLEMENTING A SCHOOL LIBRARY ONLINE COURSE

The process of implementing a school library online course at Lakeview High School in 2007 involved planning and an understanding of relevant organizational support. The Lakeview IIL was conceived as a blended course offering an online virtual learning environment through Blackboard Learning Management System and on-site practical work experience in a library setting. Students electing this course would acquire knowledge about and practical experience in library operations to enhance their lifelong personal and professional use of libraries. They would engage in project-based learning activities designed to develop twenty-first-century information literacy skills.

Beginning in 2007–2008, the Michigan Department of Education required that an experiential learning course must receive local school board approval and must be included in the student handbook or published district curriculum. The course must be part of the pupil's class schedule and must earn credit toward the pupil's high school diploma. Experiential learning courses must be taught by a certificated teacher employed by the district. In the case of a librarian's assistant course, a pupil would be required to receive curriculum-based instruction from the certificated teacher that has been approved by the local board or board of directors of a public school academy. The pupil would be given a syllabus, tests, and quizzes, and he or she would be eligible to receive credit towards a high school diploma through the issuance of a grade. In a nonlibrary example of an appropriate experiential learning course, a pupil might serve as a teacher assistant, learning teaching techniques and how to tutor or mentor other students. Once again, the course would be graded rather than pass or fail. The pupil would receive a syllabus and be evaluated through tests and quizzes.

Table 6.2.
Course overview: Introduction to information literacy

Big Ideas	Enduring Understandings	Essential Questions
Information literacy	Libraries in America, offering both traditional and electronic materials, are cornerstones of the communities they serve.	How do we learn to effectively and efficiently access and use information while also evaluating resources critically and competently?
Independent learning	Libraries provide access to the books, ideas, resources, and information that are imperative for education, employment, enjoyment, and self-government.	How can libraries encourage an appreciation of literature, a desire to independently seek information, and a commitment to lifelong learning?
Social responsibility	The online world is nearly ubiquitous in our lives, offering an incredible wealth of resources. We feel overwhelmed by this information overload and explosion of knowledge.	How can the principles of freedom of expression, intellectual property rights, and responsible technology use best be upheld?

Backward Design and Course Content

Because the IIL course contained a written curriculum that could be assessed and that adhered to Michigan Department of Education guidelines, the Lakeview Board of Education approved this course for implementation during the school year 2007–2008. The Lakeview School District's backward design process, based upon the model of Wiggins and McTighe (2001), provided a framework for curriculum work, assessment, and instruction. Criteria were identified for selecting big ideas worthy of deep understanding. Strategies were devised for framing units of study around essential questions. The course outline could be accessed from the school district website, which laid out the alignment with Michigan Educational Technology Standards (METS).

Table 6.2 highlights the big ideas, enduring understandings, and essential questions that have guided instruction. Figure 6.1 offers a summary of unit topics that support the inquiry process in the information literacy course.

Introduction and Procedures	Destiny and MeLCat	Plagiarism, Citation, Copyright
Organization and Dewey Decimal	Web Information Searches	Ethical Issues
Library as a Social Institution	Internet Safety and Netiquette	Letters About Literature
Banned Books Week	Online Databases	Teen Services
Library of Congress	Website Evaluation	Pathfinder Final Project

Figure 6.1.
Unit topics supporting inquiry process.

Course Expectations for Library Assistants

In addition to being enrolled in a course about information literacy, students would still fulfill a traditional role of being a library assistant. It was important to provide a combination of routine and challenging tasks to maximize job satisfaction (Bradshaw 2006). Each student worker therefore had an individual responsibility beyond the more mundane work of circulation duties and shelf reading. For example, one library assistant maintained book review request files, while another processed interloan items received through the library's participation in MeLCat, the statewide resource-sharing network. Student assistants took pride in their increased knowledge about library and information resources, developing a sense of ownership of the school library (Lagesten 2007). They were expected to use their time efficiently and to work independently (Schipman 2006). Job skills such as punctuality and a willingness to be of service were emphasized (Sproul 2006). Because student assistants knew that their help was greatly appreciated, they promoted the school library in a positive manner and functioned as a group of front-line library ambassadors (Yutzey 1998). Moreover, because student library assistants were taught research skills, they were better prepared to help their peers (Franklin and Stephens 2008).

Blackboard Learning Management

An essential part of the course design process was the choice of a content management system. For the first three years of implementing the online information literacy course, a decision was made to use Blackboard Learning Management. Professional development training was provided to area educators by Calhoun Intermediate School District staff. Lakeview personnel involved in online learning projects also participated in a web-based professional development course on the virtual classroom offered by LearnPort at Michigan Virtual University.[2]

Although Blackboard was utilized in the design process for IIL, an earlier prototype for the course had been piloted during the previous school year. In 2006–2007, a similar blended online/on-site course for student library assistants was set up using LearnerBlogs.

Coursework and Assignments

Following this prior successful run of the weblog-based course, IIL was officially launched with the start of the fall semester in 2007. Students enrolled in the course included three seniors and one junior, all of whom had a genuine desire to be involved in this new curricular offering in a blended online learning environment. They were curious to gain some behind-the-scenes library and research experience, which they felt would be beneficial as they continued on to college. During the first days of school (i.e., face-to-face meetings), library assistants reviewed the course syllabus and were given login instructions to access the course site. They quickly became comfortable navigating the components of Blackboard. Library assistants regularly checked the announcements section of Blackboard, which often incorporated and modeled Web 2.0 writing tools. Students then proceeded to the course documents section, where organized folders contained materials needed for completion of weekly assignments. Students

Plagiarism/ Citations

By: David Robinson

- **Plagiarism-** The uncredited use (both intentional and unintentional) of somebody else's words or ideas.
- **Punishment-** plagiarism can have severe consequences, including expulsion from a university or loss of a job, not to mention a writer's loss of credibility and professional standing
- **To Avoid-** Learn the conventions for citing documents and acknowledging sources appropriate to the field they are studying.
- **Citations-** If possible your citations should include the author, the title, the publication date and the publisher.
- **Order-** When putting your citations in the work cited page they should be in alphabetical order by the authors last name.
- **No Author?-** If there is no author for what you are citing use the first letter of the next most important information for the alphabetical order.
- **In Paper-**When citing a source in your paper, you must include the author's last name and the page number the information was found on.

Figure 6.2.
Student work.
(copyright guidelines poster)

often responded to prompts on the discussion board, engaged in online tutorials, and uploaded completed projects to the assignments section. A special effort was made to display quality work submitted by library assistants, both online via Blackboard and physically in the school library. Sample student work is depicted in Figures 6.2 and 6.3.

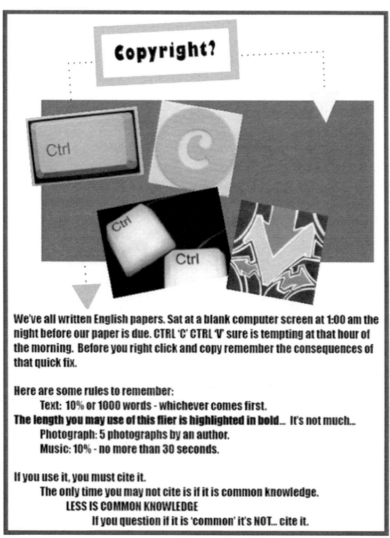

Figure 6.3.
Student work.
(copyright guidelines poster)

Course Evaluation

Student library assistants completed an online evaluation of IIL at the conclusion of the course. One survey question asked students to identify the assignment they had enjoyed the most. Students consistently selected assignments that had real-world applicability and that brought them a sense of accomplishment.

In another assignment earning high marks, students first explored the topic of book challenges by means of the ALA website and through newspaper articles documenting a series of local attempts to pull books from the shelves of Battle Creek area libraries. Students then drafted a letter to the editor of local newspaper, *The Battle Creek*

Enquirer, explaining why it is important to observe Banned Books Week (September 29–October 6, 2007) in the community. The paper published several letters on Sunday, October 7, 2007.

Students were formally assessed by means of the online tool TRAILS discussed earlier. Library assistants in fall 2007 only participated in a posttest, administered at the end of the semester, but second-semester library assistants were tested at both the start and conclusion of the spring term.

Course Modifications in 2009

During the 2009 school year, the IIL course was substantially modified. The revision was first necessary to reflect the updated software version of Blackboard 9.0. New components, icons, and functionality required that revisions be made. One of the perpetual challenges to teaching online courses is the constant change in software. As part of each weekly unit, students completed an extension to the regular assignment and recorded it in a Web 2.0 Journal. For example, after viewing a video about the networked student in week 1 (http://www.youtube.com/watch?v=XwM4ieFOotA), students created their first Web 2.0 journal entry in response to the following question: "To what extent are you a twenty-first-century student? Which tools would you like to learn more about in our course?"

Beginning in 2009, students were provided with an assessment check for each weekly unit in order for them to know how course work would be evaluated. Figure 6.4 displays a sample assessment check for the unit "Searching for Information on the Web."

An additional modification to the IIL course during the fall semester of 2009 was the inclusion of Wimba Classroom. This Blackboard component is an online collaboration tool that allows educators and students to engage in meaningful interactions by combining interactive technologies with instructional best practices. Wimba is a real-time virtual classroom environment that supports audio, video, application sharing, content display, and whiteboard. Wimba was used as part of the final project in the course and allowed students to virtually share their work.

The fall semester 2009 saw the following modifications put into place for the IIL course: a move to Blackboard 9.0, integration of Web 2.0 technology, and adherence

Expectation	Points
Effective Searching Note-Taking Guide has been uploaded to Assignments	.5
Note—Taking Guide includes 10 searching tips	1.5
Note—Taking Guide refers back to 3 online tutorials	.5
Online quiz contains 10 accurate questions about searching	1.5
Online quiz is engaging and fun for user	1.0
Online quiz has been embedded in Web 2.0 Journal	.5
Link to online slide presentation has been embedded in Web 2.0 Journal	.5

Figure 6.4.
Assessment check for unit "Searching for Information on the Web."

to AASL Standards for the 21st-Century Learner. Improvement in information literacy skills was assessed by means of TRAILS, the freely available online tool from Kent State University. Student library assistants took two different versions of TRAILS, a pretest and a posttest. Students also completed a course evaluation survey posted on the Blackboard site. In the pretest version of TRAILS given at the start of first semester of the 2009–2010 school year, students received the following scores: 24, or 75 percent, and 25, or 78 percent. On the posttest, the students scored 27, or 84 percent, and 26, or 81 percent, respectively. These scores indicate an improvement in information literacy skills among students in the IIL course that was modified for the fall semester of 2009.

The TRAILS administrative site further permits a breakdown of information literacy skills by category. A noticeable improvement occurred in the category "Evaluate sources and information," with the percentage increase going from 69 percent on the pretest to 81 percent on the posttest. This TRAILS category figured in week 10's unit on website evaluation, which was also rated as a favorite assignment by information literacy students in the end-of-semester evaluation survey. After completing their own week 10 work, information literacy students went into another Lakeview High School course (Cultural Literacy) and taught mini-lessons to fellow students about website evaluation (Lincoln 2010).

DISSEMINATING A SCHOOL LIBRARY ONLINE COURSE EXPERIENCE

How has it been possible to connect with both school librarians and classroom teachers so that other educators can benefit from one school library's venture into online learning? The dissemination process has been carried out through several measures, including the creation of a professional development wiki (http://remc12.wikispaces. com/). Blackboard training has been offered to high school teachers. Collaborative online instructional projects have been developed by school librarian and classroom teachers. Lakeview teachers have partnered with and received support from a Wayne State University researcher who is studying the implementation of Michigan's online learning requirement. Input and materials about school libraries' involvement in online learning have been obtained from school librarians by means of a questionnaire posted on several listservs. Finally, a call for action and continued involvement in online learning on the part of school library professionals has been put forth.

Blackboard Training for Classroom Teachers

Part of the dissemination process for the school library's venture into online learning involved providing Blackboard training to classroom teachers at Lakeview High School. A decision had been made that Lakeview students would fulfill the 20-hour online learning graduation requirement through the semester-long economics course taken by all eleventh graders. It was therefore necessary to offer professional development for the economics teachers. During the 2008–2009 school year, the school librarian provided two full-day professional development sessions, giving instruction in Blackboard and assistance in setting up course sites. Follow-up sessions for economics teachers were provided in 2009–2010 to acquaint teachers with new features of Blackboard 9.0.

As economics teachers developed an online platform for delivering instruction, student achievement was monitored. An attempt was made to determine whether students performed better on curricular units that have been modified to reflect best practice in technology integration. Because Lakeview High School had set data analysis as an ongoing school improvement goal and because teachers were using the program Data Director in this project, results were compared on cumulative unit assessments (CUAs). Figure 6.5 shows an online unit transformation template, which served as a guide for effectively integrating technology into an existing unit. The template called for a description of the involvement of the school library in the transformation of the unit through direct instruction and provision of resources.

Collaborative Online Instructional Projects

Along with making professional development available, the school librarian worked with fellow teachers to incorporate various online activities from the ILL Blackboard

Course and Unit	Type existing course and specific unit here.	
Files	Give links to supporting files on school district server.	
Overview	Give a brief overview of existing unit. How does the unit address enduring understandings or essential questions?	
Content standards	List here content standards and benchmarks addressed by this unit.	
Exemplary course ideas/links	Note ideas/links from Online Learning page of the REMC 12 wiki that may be used in updating existing unit (http://remc12.wikispaces.com/Online+Learning).	
Information literacy	List research skills practice that may be incorporated into this lesson through resources listed on the Information Literacy page of the REMC 12 wiki (http://remc12.wikispaces.com/Information+Literacy).	
Lesson plan resources	Include possible instructional activities supporting meaningful online learning that may be adapted and found through the Lesson Development page of the REMC 12 wiki (http://remc12.wikispaces.com/Lesson+Development).	
Web 2.0 resources	Explore the Web 2.0 page of the REMC 12 wiki to suggest resources to incorporate into unit (http://remc12.wikispaces.com/Web+2.0).	
Library Media Center	Describe involvement of the school library media center in this unit through direct instruction and provision of resources.	
Data analysis	A comparison of results on CUA before and after online unit transformation:	
	Pre–unit transformation CUA	Post–unit transformation CUA
	Provide link to pre–unit transformation School Exam Report on Data Director.	Provide link to post–unit transformation School Exam Report on Data Director.

Figure 6.5.
Online unit transformation template.

course into instructional units taught in other academic departments at Lakeview High School. For example, students in the ILL course learned how to set up Blogline accounts. Students in the economics course then engaged in a similar project, which was co-taught with the classroom teacher. Students created aggregators to bring in news feeds and search alerts from the library's subscription databases. A short library presentation on how to use Bloglines was uploaded to TeacherTube and linked to from the Economics Blackboard site.

Although the use of Blackboard as a content management system for delivering economics curriculum was a primary focus, the school librarian also worked with other Lakeview teachers to help them set up online course sites. A new course, Cultural Literacy, debuted at Lakeview High School in the 2009–2010 school year and utilized Blackboard, as shown in Figure 6.6. The school librarian teamed with the classroom teacher in delivering instruction and also assumed an online presence as an embedded librarian in the course site, responding to students' research questions. As noted, ILL students were invited into the cultural literacy course to teach mini-lessons to fellow students on website evaluation.

Partnering with Wayne State University

To further Lakeview's ability to obtain valuable support and professional development related to online learning in these difficult economic times, contact was established with Dr. Michael Barbour, a professor of instructional technology, a researcher at Wayne State University, and moderator of the previously cited Virtual High School Meanderings blog. Dr. Barbour began advising economics teachers, observing their online course sites and suggesting appropriate materials to incorporate into instruction. Dr. Barbour was especially interested in how Lakeview teachers were implementing

Figure 6.6.
Cultural Literacy Blackboard site.

Michigan's twenty-hour online learning graduation requirement in a blended or hybrid course. Dr. Barbour constructed a survey of Lakeview High School students to be used in his research that examines how best to support students enrolled in online courses.

School Library Online Learning Questionnaire

As stated earlier, the increase in online learning projects is well-documented in the literature. However, fewer studies have examined the involvement of school libraries in this growing trend. In an attempt to gather input from school librarians who have used a course content management system to teach an online course in a K–12 setting, a questionnaire was set up on a secure site of the Lakeview District server. The questionnaire announcement was posted on the following listservs: LM_NET, American Association of School Librarians (AASL) Forum, International Association of School Libraries (IASL), and Michigan Association of Media in Education (MAME). See https://secure.schoolworld.com/formsTP/forms.cfm?myform=12051&DSID=63&teacher=23062.

The response rate generated by postings to these listservs was not strong. A total of twenty-one respondents completed the questionnaire from among thousands of members of the listservs. One of the largest, LM_NET, has more than 12,000 subscribers (LM_NET 2010); AASL has 700, and IASL has an additional 500. The low response rate could suggest that very few school librarians are currently engaged in online learning. Nevertheless, some of the questionnaire responses are summarized here.

Geographical distribution included thirteen fourteen respondents from Michigan, three respondents from Canada (British Columbia), and single respondents from Georgia, Missouri, New Jersey, and Wisconsin. There were nineteen respondents at the secondary level (high school or middle school); one respondent at the K–12 level; and one respondent at the college level.

Respondents gave various reasons for having become involved in online learning. Most cited having taken an online course for their own graduate work as an impetus to develop an online course for students, but another listed a desire to acquaint middle and high school students with the skills needs to be a successful online learner. The use of an online course site let one school librarian balance the demands of combining a flexible library schedule with teaching classes on a fixed schedule.

Professional development opportunities have helped prepare respondents to teach online. School librarians mentioned that many courses taken in recent years to maintain certification have been conducted online, thereby affording online literacy and a comfort level with this form of instruction. They also reported that their university degrees included web training and online course experience. Training provided by local school districts, intermediate or regional districts, state organizations, and conferences was further identified as valuable for professional development.

Some respondents reported that technical and instructional support was available for their online course at the school-district level. Respondents mentioned being their own source of help and that they support other colleagues. Several respondents claimed to be their own teacher and problem solver.

Blackboard was the course content management system most frequently in use by a school district, followed by Moodle. Costs associated with running these systems were covered at the local, intermediate, or regional district level. In other instances, however, the management system required minimal funding because an open-source product such as Moodle was being utilized. Web 2.0 applications such as WordPress, blogging software, and wikis were other no-cost or low-cost alternatives.

A related question asked respondents to identify an online instructional activity that students found particularly engaging within the online course. Among others, respondents reported that students enjoyed various Web 2.0 applications. Video blogs, YouTube, Animoto, and Dipity received high marks. Students were drawn to multimedia project components that offered choice.

When asked to list five supplemental Web 2.0 tools (e.g., social networking sites, podcasting, RSS, image generators, cloud computing) that had been incorporated into their online course, some respondents indicated that such tools were blocked by their school district's server. A number of people, however, identified the following supplemental Web 2.0 tools: Weebly, Blogger, Wikispaces, YouTube, Teachertube, Flickr, Dabbleboard, Wordle, Quizlet, Animoto, PhotoPeach, Mister-Wong, and Screencasts. Respondents also reported having used Adobe Buzzword, Drop.io, FlySuite, iNetWord Editor, j2e.com, Microsoft Office Live, Nevrocode Docs, OpenOffice.org, Peepel, Solodox, ThinkFree, Google Docs, Google Sites, Writeboard, Zoho Office Suite, PBworks, WordPress, CamStudio, Camtasia Studio, Jing, Audacity, Picasa 3, JayCut, Viddler.com, and Vimeo.

School library professionals are assuming an important role in growing phenomenon of K–12 online learning. The survey respondents had co-taught or participated in online courses taught by teacher colleagues. School librarians often take responsibility for troubleshooting technical problems associated with online course management. In addition to going directly into a classroom to teach a mini-lesson or unit in a colleague's blended online course, respondents mentioned assisting other instructors in generating materials for their course websites. One respondent even spoke of having created an "e-library" for online courses and working with teachers from every faculty to design new research-based assignments that serve to familiarize students with this library of digital resources. School librarians are beginning to recognize their vital connection to online learning. Involvement in existing online courses and development of future curricular offerings may gain school librarians some job security and will allow them to assume an essential role in twenty-first-century education. Additional comments are shared below in Table 6.3 with permission of the respondents:

While this study had the potential of many respondents, the few who did answer likely reflect the general perceptions of school librarians on online instruction. The field is in its infancy, and as it grows and more research is conducted, a better picture should emerge.

Call for Action and Ongoing Involvement of School Library Professionals in Online Learning

School librarians need to begin showing an interest in and a commitment to online learning, to become involved in this developing component of K–12 education. As school librarians advocate for school librarianship as a profession and provide compelling data as to how they positively affect teaching and learning, their role in online education must not be overlooked. Along with regular classroom teachers, school librarians should contribute to professional publications and offer conference presentations about their experience in online learning (Lincoln 2008; Lincoln 2009a; Lincoln 2009b; Lincoln 2010).

Table 6.3.

School librarians' role in online learning

Comments
School librarians and library personnel should be on the forefront of this type of technology and provide support to their entire environment. Especially as budgets shrink, this can be a great way to continue reaching a wide audience.
Online learning provides an excellent opportunity for school librarians to provide service-oriented courses (such as media, office, and teacher assistant positions), along with other courses that fit into the school librarian's area of certification. School librarians can also serve as school mentors for online education.
School librarians have an instrumental role to play in online education. We are the lighthouses that help illuminate the way for our students and teacher colleagues to navigate the wide expansive sea of information.
School librarians are being more responsible for monitoring of the cloud classroom environments of the future. They will be the keepers of the online repositories for global information to the students and staff.
The school librarian's role as an online reference librarian could be quite beneficial for students. If students could directly contact school librarians through the course management system for research-related questions, librarians could help instill vital lifelong learning skills. They should also support teachers in learning and in teaching students to use the course management system.
If administrators are willing, the school librarian can be the hub for online learning. It is exciting to be on the edge with each class.

Heisey and Thom (2007) concur that a key component of any successful school library program is the formation of partnerships. Rather than working in isolation, a school librarian must reach out to colleagues and collaboratively design, teach, and evaluate units of instruction. School librarians must be partners in the educational process if they want to play an integral role in curriculum development, instruction, and assessment. In the new online learning environment, school librarians are creating an infrastructure to support the dynamic and evolving ways that students and teachers use information resources. School librarians must work to achieve meaningful learning and information literacy in the virtual realm.

NOTES

1. *CareerForward*, http://www.mivhs.org/Careers/CareerForward/tabid/273/Default.aspx.
2. *LearnPort*, http://mi.learnport.org/.

REFERENCES

Abilock, Debbie. 2005. "Homepage. We're Here! Great Digital Teacher-Librarians." *Knowledge Quest* 34 (1): 8–10.
Adolphus, Margaret. 2009. "Using the Web to Teach Information Literacy." *Online* 33 (4): 20–25.

American Association of School Librarians. 2007. "Standards for the 21st-Century Learner." Accessed July 30, 2011. http://ala.org/ala/mgrps/divs/aasl/guidelinesandstandards/learningstandards/AASL_LearningStandards.pdf.

Appleton, Karen, Dorothy DeGroot, Karen Lampe, and Cheryl Carruth. 2009. "How Rural School Librarians Stay Connected." *School Library Monthly* 26 (2): 14–16.

Archambault, Leanna, and Kent Crippen. 2009. "K–12 Distance Educators at Work: Who's Teaching Online Across the United States." *Journal of Research on Technology in Education* 41 (4): 363–91.

Armstrong, Sara. 2007. "Virtual Learning 2.0: Professional Development is a Whole New Ballgame for Educators Who Teach Online." *Technology & Learning* 28 (4): 26–29.

Battle, Joel C. 2007. "Information Literacy Instruction for Educators and the Role of School and Academic Libraries." *Texas Library Journal* 83 (3): 120–12, 124–25.

Bauer, John, and Jeffrey Kenton. 2005. "Toward Technology Integration in the Schools: Why It Isn't Happening." *Journal of Technology and Teacher Education* 13 (4): 519–46.

Bradford, Peter, Margaret Porciello, Nancy Balkon, and Debra Backus. 2007. "The Blackboard Learning System: The Be All and End All in Educational Instruction?" *Journal of Educational Technology Systems* 35 (3): 301–14.

Bradshaw, Maria C. 2006. "Keep Your Student Workers." *Library Journal (1976)* 131 (19): 44.

British Library. 2008. "Information Behaviour of the Researcher of the Future." Accessed July 28, 2011. http://www.jisc.ac.uk/media/documents/programmes/reppres/ggworkpackageii.pdf.

Brown, Cecelia, Teri J. Murphy, and Mark Nanny. 2003. "Turning Techno-Savvy into Info-Savvy: Authentically Integrating Information Literacy into the College Curriculum." *The Journal of Academic Librarianship* 29 (6): 386–98.

Cahoy, Ellysa Stern. 2004. "Put Some Feeling into It!: Integrating Affective Competencies into K–20 Information Literacy Standards." *Knowledge Quest* 32 (4): 25–28.

Dando, Priscille M. 2005. "First Steps in Online Learning: Creating an Environment for Instructional Support and Assessment." *Knowledge Quest* 34 (1): 23–24.

Esch, Carrie, and Amy Crawford. 2006. "Helping Students Make the Jump to University Level Research." *MultiMedia & Internet@Schools* 13 (2): 21–24.

Evergreen Group. 2009. *Keeping Pace with K–12 Online Learning.* Accessed July 28, 2011. http://www.kpk12.com/wp-content/uploads/KeepingPace09-fullreport.pdf.

"Fast Facts About Online Learning." 2010. International North American Council for Online Learning. Accessed July 28, 2011. http://www.inacol.org/press/docs/nacol_fast_facts.pdf.

Franklin, Pat, and Claire Gatrell Stephens. 2008. "Student Assistants: Helpers and Learners!" *School Library Media Activities Monthly* 24 (9): 43–44.

Fredrick, Kathy. 2009. "Stay the Course. Managing Online Presence." *School Library Monthly* 26 (2): 33–34.

Giles, Kara L. 2004. "Reflections on a Privilege." *College & Research Libraries News* 65 (5): 261–68.

Guhlin, Miguel. 2009. "*Moodle*™-izing Your Education Environment." Education World. Accessed July 31, 2011. http://www.education-world.com/a_tech/columnists/guhlin/guhlin012.shtml.

Heisey, Beth A., and Margaret Thom. 2007. "Partnership or Collaboration? It's Both in Bakersfield." *CSLA Journal* 30 (2): 33–34.

Herring, Susan D., Robert R. Burkhardt, and Jennifer L. Wolfe. 2009. "Reaching Remote Students." *College & Research Libraries News* 70 (11): 630–33.

Jackson, Pamela Alexandra. 2007. "Integrating Information Literacy into Blackboard: Building Campus Partnerships for Successful Student Learning." *The Journal of Academic Librarianship* 33 (4): 454–61.

Kachel, Debra E., Nancy L. Henry, and Cynthia A. Keller. 2005. "Making It Real Online: Distance Learning for High School Students." *Knowledge Quest* 34 (1): 14–17.

Kowitt, Beth. 2009. "Blackboard Rules the Schools." *Fortune* 160 (9): 28.

Lagesten, Carin E. 2007. "Students as Library Leaders: Student Team Builds Leadership Skills While Helping to Battle Budget Cuts." *Teacher Librarian* 34 (5): 45–47.

Lang, James M. 2007. "Midterm Grades for Blackboard." *The Chronicle of Higher Education* 54 (13): C2–C3.

Lincoln, Margaret. 2010. "Information Evaluation and Online Coursework." *Knowledge Quest* 38 (3): 28–31.

Lincoln, Margaret. 2009a. "Information Literacy: An Online Library Media Course for High School Students." Presentation given at the American Association of School Librarians 14th National Conference and Exhibition, Charlotte, North Carolina, November 6, 2009.

Lincoln, Margaret. 2009b. "Information Literacy: An Online Course for Student Library Assistants." *School Library Media Activities Monthly* 25 (10): 29–30.

Lincoln, Margaret. 2008. "Introduction to Information Literacy: An Online Library Media Course for High School Students." Paper presented at International Association of School Librarianship, Berkeley, California, August 4, 2008.

List, Jonathan S., and Brent Bryant. 2009. "Integrating Interactive Online Content at an Early College High School: An Exploration of Moodle, Ning and Twitter." *Meridian: A Middle School Computer Technologies Journal* 12 (1). Accessed July 28, 2011. http://www.ncsu.edu/meridian/winter2009/List/index.htm.

LM_NET@LISTSERV.SYR.EDU. 2010. "School Library Media and Network Communications." Accessed July 31, 2011. http://www.lsoft.com/scripts/wl.exe?SL1=LM_NET&H=LISTSERV.SYR.EDU.

Matthew, Victoria, and Ann Schroeder. 2006. "The Embedded Librarian Program." *Educause Quarterly* 29 (4). Accessed July 31, 2011. http://www.educause.edu/ir/library/pdf/eqm06410.pdf.

Menges, Beth. 2009. "Using Moodle (Open Source Software) with Grades 3–6." *School Library Monthly* 26 (2): 21–22.

Michigan Department of Education. 2006. *Michigan Merit Curriculum Guidelines*. Accessed July 29, 2011. http://www.michigan.gov/documents/mde/Online10.06_final_175750_7.pdf.

Novotny, Eric, and Ellysa Stern Cahoy. 2006. "If We Teach, Do They Learn? The Impact of Instruction on Online Catalog Search Strategies." *Libraries and the Academy* 6 (2): 155–167.

Owens, Rachel. 2008. "Where the Students Are: The Embedded Librarian Project at Daytona Beach College." *Florida Libraries* 51 (1): 8–10.

Pappas, Marjorie. 2005. "Guest Editor's Column." *Knowledge Quest* 34 (1): 11–12.

Ramsay, Karen M., and Jim Kinnie. 2006. "The Embedded Librarian." *Library Journal* 131 (6): 34–35.

Richardson, Will. 2007. "Online-Powered School Libraries." *District Administration* 43 (1): 62–63.

Rohland-Heinrich, Nancy, and Brian Jensen. 2007. "Library Resources: A Critical Component to Online Learning." *MultiMedia & Internet@Schools* 14 (2): 8–12.

Schloman, Barbara F., and Julie A. Gedeon. 2007. "Creating TRAILS: Tool for Real-Time Assessment of Information Literacy Skills." *Knowledge Quest* 35 (5): 44–47.

Schipman, Mavis. 2006. "It's Cool to Work in the Library . . . Student Library Aides." *Library Media Connection* 25 (3): 26–27.

Scott, Thomas J., and Michael K. O'Sullivan. 2005. "Analyzing Student Search Strategies: Making a Case for Integrating Information Literacy Skills into the Curriculum." *Teacher Librarian* 33 (1): 21–25.

Sproul, Betty. 2006. "Implementing a Library Helper Program Is Easy, An Economical, and Energizing." *Library Media Connection* 24 (7): 44–46.

Tallman, Julie, and Mary Ann Fitzgerald. 2005. "Blending Online and Classroom Learning Environments: Reflections on Experiences and Points to Consider." *Knowledge Quest* 34 (1): 25–28.

Tipton, Molly. "*Moodle*™ in the Classroom." Accessed July 28, 2011. http://www.teachertube.com/viewVideo.php?video_id=10010.

Trotter, Andrew. 2008. "Market for K–12 Course-Management Systems Expands." *Education Digest* 73 (9): 17–20.

U.S. Department of Education. 2004. *National Education Technology Plan 2004*. Accessed July 29, 2011. http://www.ed.gov/about/offices/list/os/technology/plan/2004/plan.pdf.

U.S. Department of Education. 2010. *DRAFT National Educational Technology Plan 2010*. Accessed July 29, 2011. http://www.ed.gov/sites/default/files/NETP-2010-final-report.pdf.

West, Richard, Greg Waddoups, and Charles Graham. 2007. "Understanding the Experiences of Instructors as They Adopt a Course Management System." *Educational Technology Research & Development* 55 (1): 1–26.

Wiggins, Grant, and Jay McTighe. 2001. *Understanding by Design*. Upper Saddle River, NJ: Merrill/Prentice Hall.

Yohe, Paula. 2007. "Getting Information Literacy Standards Noticed: How Promoting These Standards Just Might Save Your Job." *Library Media Connection* 26 (3): 28–30.

York, Amy C., and Jason M. Vance. 2009. "Taking Library Instruction into the Online Classroom: Best Practices for Embedded Librarians." *Journal of Library Administration* 49 (1/2): 197–209.

Yutzey, Susan D. 1998. "The Evolution of a School Library Volunteer Program." *Ohio Media Spectrum* 50 (2): 33–35.

Index

About the Editors and Contributors

Susan W. Alman is director of online education at the School of Information Sciences, University of Pittsburgh. She specializes in asynchronous learning, marketing and PR for libraries, and interpersonal communication. Alman received her BA from Washington and Jefferson College and her MLS and PhD from the University of Pittsburgh. Tomer and Alman worked with Mary K. Biagini to design and implement the first online degree program offered at the University of Pittsburgh.

Barbara A. Frey, is a teaching and learning consultant at the Center for Instructional Development and Distance Education, University of Pittsburgh. She specializes in online teaching and learning, instructional design and technology, and web accessibility. Frey received her DEd in adult education from Pennsylvania State University. In addition to her position at the University of Pittsburgh, Dr. Frey teaches as an adjunct assistant professor in the Learning and Performance Systems Department of Pennsylvania State University World Campus and as an instructor with the Online Teaching and Learning Program of Colorado State University's Global Campus. Dr. Frey is also a master reviewer and trainer with Quality Matters, a nonprofit organization that promotes quality in online courses.

Arianne Hartsell-Gundy is humanities librarian at Miami University in Ohio and liaison to English, Theatre, and Communication. Her research areas include information literacy, graduate student instruction, and digital humanities. Hartsell-Gundy received her MLS/MA in comparative literature from Indiana University and her BA in English from University of Missouri-Columbia.

Lorna R. Kearns, is a teaching and learning consultant at the Center for Instructional Development and Distance Education, University of Pittsburgh. In her work, she consults with faculty on teaching and learning issues, conducts faculty development workshops, and works with faculty to develop online courses. She has taught both face-to-face and online and has administered online programs at Carnegie Mellon University. Kearns received her BA in Linguistics and MS in Information Science from the University of Pittsburgh.

Margaret L. Lincoln is the district librarian for Lakeview Schools in Battle Creek, Michigan. She earned a PhD in library and information sciences from the University of North Texas in 2006. Margaret has contributed professional articles to *The Book Report*, *Knowledge Quest*, *Library Media Connection*, *Media Spectrum*, *Multi Media Schools*, and *School Library Journal*. Her research interests focus on online vs. onsite Holocaust museum exhibitions as informational resources. Margaret is the elected Michigan school library representative on the Midwest Collaborative for Library Services board. She received the Ruby Brown Award for Individual Excellence from MAME in 2000 and the 2004 AASL Collaborative School Library Media Award. In 2008, Margaret was one of ten librarians nationwide selected as a recipient of the Carnegie Corporation of New York/New York Times I Love My Librarian Award. At the March 2012 MACUL Conference, she was honored with the coveted ISTE Making It Happen award for her contributions to the successful integration of technology in education in K–12 schools.

Kelly Otter is associate dean of Graduate Academic and Faculty Affairs for the College of Professional Studies, Northeastern University. Her areas of specialization include academic and technology-mediated program development; adult student enrollment management through strategic marketing, recruitment, and prospect cultivation; retention of adult students; cultivation of internal and external partnerships (including community colleges, government, and nonprofit entities) for curriculum development and delivery; staff management and development; and program assessment and evaluation. Otter received her MA from Wayne State University and her PhD from New York University.

Christinger Tomer is an associate professor at the School of Information Sciences, University of Pittsburgh. He specializes in digital libraries, library and archival computing, and online education. Tomer received his BA from the College of Wooster and an MLS and PhD from Case Western Reserve University. Tomer and Alman worked with Mary K. Biagini to design and implement the first online degree program offered at the University of Pittsburgh.

Beth Tumbleson is assistant director of the Gardner-Harvey Library, Miami University Middletown. Her areas of specialization and experience include information literacy, LMS-embedded librarianship, distance learning, 12–13 transition from high school to college libraries and research, and electronic resources. Tumbleson received her MS in library science from Simmons College in Boston, Massachusetts. She has worked as an academic, school, and corporate librarian. Most recently, she has co-presented at such national conferences as LOEX, ACRL, Distance Library Services, and LITA National Forum as well as published on LMS-embedded librarianship.

Edwards Brothers Malloy
Thorofare, NJ USA
July 18, 2012